Horse Care and Stable Management

HORSE CARE

and

STABLE MANAGEMENT

Marcy Drummond

The Crowood Press

First published in 1988 by
The Crowood Press Ltd
Ramsbury, Marlborough
Wiltshire SN8 2HR

This impression 1995

British Library Cataloguing-in-Publication Data

A catalogue record for this book is available from
the British Library.

ISBN 1 85223 712 0

Picture Credits
Line illustrations by Elaine How.

Acknowledgements
Many people have contributed to the production of this book,
most of them unwittingly, as they provided such knowledge that
I have accumulated over the years. In particular I would like to
thank Peter Jeffrey of *Horse and Hound*, Tony Pavord, MRCVS,
and most of all my parents, Pat and Bill Wedlake, for their help
and patience.

Typeset by Action Typesetting Ltd, Gloucester
Printed in Great Britain by The Bath Press

Contents

Introduction

'He's forgotten more about horses than most of us will ever know.' How often have you heard that statement made about a knowledgeable and venerated horseman? As you will soon come to realise, if you have very much to do with horses, it is true that the more you learn, the more you find there is to learn — the process of discovery and enlightenment is unending. If you have been bitten by the 'horse bug', it is also a process that is both fascinating and rewarding.

The purpose of this book, therefore, is not to try to tell you everything there is to know about horses and how to look after them, but to dispel some of the mystery surrounding successful horse management, to look at both traditional and modern methods of horse keeping and, above all, to provide practical help and information on caring for a horse, or horses, on a day-to-day basis.

1 . Buying a Horse

ASSESSING YOUR NEEDS

The way you look after your horse will be determined by several different factors: what type of horse he is, how old he is, how advanced your riding is, what you plan to do with him, and the facilities you have at your disposal. These must all be considered before you go out and buy a horse. The wrong type of horse for his owner, kept in an unsuitable environment for that particular horse, is a recipe for disaster. One of the most common problems is that the prospective horse owner has in mind a picture of a striking looking horse that attracts the eye, either fine and pretty or big, powerful and impressive. Horses like these are unsuitable for anyone who has never owned a horse before. The great day dawns, the horse arrives and almost immediately the problems begin. The new owner finds he not only has difficulty in riding the horse, but also in handling him in the stable.

Perhaps the horse lays back his ears and bares his teeth when the owner approaches the stable; perhaps he won't stand still to be groomed or tacked up, or perhaps he tries to kick. He may try to charge out of the box whenever the door is opened, or to rush ahead when led. In fact, the highly bred horse's powers of invention to frustrate an inexperienced handler are endless.

An experienced owner, on the other hand, will know exactly how to cope with these difficulties and how far the horse may be allowed to express his character before he becomes a nuisance. Later we will consider some ways of dealing with these problems, but at this point let us consider the type of horse a first-time owner should buy.

Horse's Age and Size

There are certainly some horses an inexperienced owner should not buy if he intends to have a horse to ride who will give years of lasting pleasure.

Fig 1 Future racehorses bred in Kentucky. Foals are appealing, but need time, patience and expert handling to bring them to successful maturity.

Many people buy a foal or yearling, believing that they can learn as the youngster grows up; such animals are also often inexpensive. This is mistake number one. The horse will not be ridable until he is at least three years old. In the mean time, and during his early training, he must be well fed and properly handled, all of which entails time and expense without riding. Backing and schooling a young horse are jobs for an experienced rider.

The minimum age for a horse to begin serious work is five years old, and then he should be brought on lightly for another year or two. So if you are looking for your first horse, make seven or eight the minimum age limit.

The horse has two sets of teeth — temporary and permanent. The temporary teeth are progressively replaced by the permanent teeth at the ages of two and a half, three and a half, and four and a half, so it is quite easy to establish a young horse's age by looking at his teeth. At the age of five all the permanent teeth are present and thereafter age is determined by the state of wear. The teeth grow and are worn down continuously through the horse's life. The central incisors wear

first, followed by the lateral and corner incisors. A new tooth has a hollow (or infundibulum) in the centre, which is gradually worn away and replaced by a brown stain called the 'dental star'.

At seven years a hook appears on the corner incisors, which disappears at eight. At ten a groove, known as Galvayne's groove, starts to appear at the top of the corner incisors. By the age of twenty this has reached the bottom and starts to grow out. The shape of the teeth also changes, becoming more sloping and elongated as the horse grows older. The wearing surfaces change from oral to round and finally triangular in shape. From the age of eight the changes in the teeth are less obvious and less accurately timed; assessing the horse's age in this way becomes more difficult.

You want to be able to enjoy your horse for some time, or perhaps sell him when you have gained more experience. Horses begin to slow down in their teens, although many go on working and competing into their twenties. The value of a horse tends to fall, in relation to his age, once he reaches the age of twelve. If you can find a horse between the ages of eight and twelve, therefore, you will pay a little more for him, but have more use from him than from an older horse. On the other hand, many horses retire from competing to make excellent schoolmasters for less experienced riders, and provided you give some thought to what will happen to the horse when he is no longer up to what you want from him, such a horse could be a good initial buy.

Next, consider yourself — your height and weight, your experience, or lack of it, of handling horses as well as of riding them, your level of ability and confidence, your aims and ambitions, and what you want to achieve from your relationship with a horse. There is an unfortunate idea in some horsy circles nowadays that anyone over the age of 16, or over about 5ft 6in (1m 65cm) tall, needs a horse of at least 16hh. That is one reason why the extra inches on a horse from 16hh. upwards seem to cost so much more, *pro rata*, than the rest of him. The other reason is that bigger horses, particularly for eventing and hunting, are supposed to have more scope for jumping big fences than smaller horses. This may

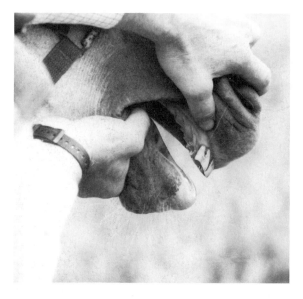

Fig 2 A seven-year hook, quite clearly visible on this horse's upper corner incisor.

be true, but is not exclusively the case. Charisma, the gold medal-winning event horse ridden by tall New Zealander Mark Todd is only 15.3hh., Marion Mould's top showjumper, Stroller, was just a pony at 14.2hh., and the world's greatest steeplechase, the Grand National, has been won by horses tiny by today's standards. Battleship, ridden to victory by Bruce Hobbs in 1938, at odds against of 40-1, was barely 15.2hh.

Your weight is more important than your height, and the shape of the horse you buy more important than his height. The essential point is to co-ordinate rider and horse. A tall, heavy man is unlikely to feel very comfortable on a show hack (never mind what the hack might think of it!), but he might well feel quite at home on a strong, solid cob who is, nevertheless, no taller than the hack.

You may be in a situation where more than one person is going to ride the horse, perhaps your whole family, at different times and in different spheres. Of course in this case any horse's

development as a specialist will be limited by the necessity to choose an all-rounder who, for example, can be hunted, jumped, shown and 'Pony Clubbed'. A willing cob or native cross is often the best choice for this job.

Breed

If you have local showjumping, hunter trials or other competitions in mind, have had some riding lessons, and are reasonably confident of your ability to handle a horse, you will need an active, willing type who can carry you well, but is not highly strung and excitable. A part-bred is the best choice here, that is a cross between a Thoroughbred (the English Thoroughbred is the breed developed for racing) and some other breed. The other breed could be one of the British native pony breeds, a foreign breed, or a mixture, but native pony crosses do make excellent riding horses. The larger breeds, such as the Connemara, Welsh Cob, Fell, Dales, or Highland

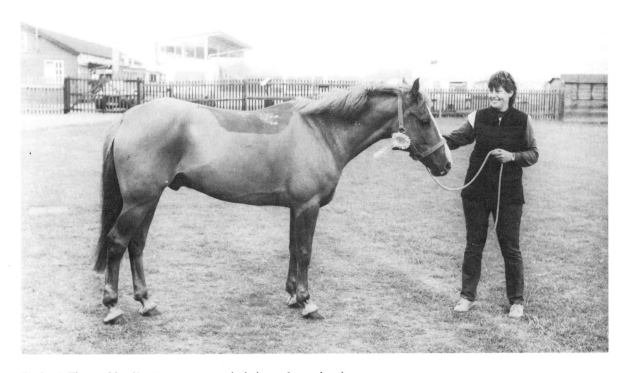

Fig 3   A Thoroughbred/native cross — an ideal choice for a riding horse.

Fig 4   Shilstone Rocks Another Bunch is a top prize-winning Dartmoor pony
brood mare and shows all the best qualities of her type.

are the obvious ones, the Connemara being
favoured for its looks, as it is a lighter-boned,
more elegant pony, and the Welsh Cob for its
keen temperament. Of the smaller breeds, the
Dartmoor makes an excellent cross with the
Thoroughbred, to produce a small horse of
Thoroughbred type; the ideal Dartmoor is often
described as a 'miniature Thoroughbred'.

The one cross you should not consider as a first
horse is that of the Thoroughbred with the Arab,
known as the Anglo-Arab. The Thoroughbred
and the Arab are the two breeds referred to as 'hot
blooded', the former, in fact, deriving from the
latter. Some 'blood' is desirable in all
competition horses, to provide courage and
speed, but both breeds need expert handling and
the Anglo-Arab is an extremely sharp, sensitive
horse who should be left to the experienced
horseman.

Second and third crosses with Thoroughbreds
to produce three-quarter or seven-eighths bred
horses are also popular for eventers and
showjumpers. Just remember that the greater the
proportion of Thoroughbred blood, the more
sensitive the horse, the livelier the ride and the
quicker his reactions.

How much weight can a horse carry? There is
no absolute rule, but, in general, the lighter-
framed the horse, the less he will comfortably
carry. Pure Thoroughbreds and Arabs are bred for
speed, so they tend to be lightly built, hence the
demand for part-breds for competition work and
hunting. In fact, Arab horses have fewer
vertebrae than other breeds, giving them a short,
strong back which enables them to carry
considerable weight in relation to their size.
However, in the past there has been some
prejudice against the use of Arabs in breeding

10

Fig 5 Bred for speed — top Thoroughbred stud Seattle Slew, at his Kentucky home.

competition horses and riding horses, probably because of their quick intelligence which needs careful handling. Nevertheless, there are many Arab crosses working successfully in all spheres of equestrianism, although the Arabian influence on their breeding is often conveniently forgotten.

Native ponies are very strong and even the small breeds are capable, within reason, of carrying adults without difficulty. Most part-bred horses will carry up to 12 stone (76.2kg) with comparative ease; above that you will probably need to consider a mount of 16hh. plus. Remember, it is not just your actual weight that counts, but how it is distributed when you are riding. It is much easier for a horse to carry a fit, well-balanced rider, than an unfit, overweight, unbalanced rider, even if they both weigh exactly the same.

Some riders are blessed with perfect riding conformation — a slim frame, with an upper body not too long and proportionately long legs. Most of us are less lucky and if you are buying your own horse, you might as well buy one that is as well suited to your physical shape as to your other requirements. Therefore, don't buy a rotund, cobby type of horse if you are short, with short legs — riding will be hard work, with too much effort spent in simply maintaining an effective riding position. Look for a narrower type. Similarly, if you are tall, a short horse may well cope with your weight, but you may feel unbalanced and uncomfortably top heavy.

Temperament

When you buy your new horse you will be thinking mainly about riding, but the way he behaves when you are on the ground is just as

11

Fig 6   An ideal child's pony, but the Dartmoor can easily carry a light adult.
These ponies were originally bred by farmers for herding stock on the moor.

important. You will be buying a made horse and his manners in the stable, or when being led and handled, should be as calm and amenable as when you are on his back. Teaching a horse good stable manners is part of his early training and if this has been neglected it is quite likely that other aspects of his schooling have suffered too. Watch how he behaves with his current owner, then handle him yourself if you feel happy to do so (if not, don't buy him). Run your hands over him, pick up his feet, watch when he is tacked up, or do it yourself, lead him out of his box, trot him up in hand, see him loaded — these are all reasonable things to expect to see and do before you commit yourself to buying a horse. Ask how he behaves when being clipped and shod, and when visited by the vet, and make a note of the reply you are given. Ask if he has any of the common stable vices such as crib-biting, wind-sucking or weaving, and, again, make a note of what you are told. Find out as

much as you can about your prospective purchase, including his past history, number of owners, how he has been kept (stabled or at grass?) and ask about his likes as well as his dislikes. The more you know about your horse when you first get him home, the easier it should be to understand him and to manage him successfully.

Environment

The final consideration before you choose your horse is how you are going to keep him. The back garden is not, as some people seem to think, the best place. Your horse will need stabling and pasture — in what measure will be discussed later — and you must consider whether the facilities you have available are suitable for the type of horse you have in mind. A pony can live out, with adequate grazing, supplemented as necessary, and a field shelter. Most horses can also live out most

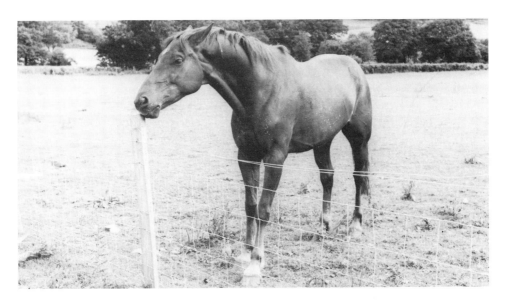

Fig 7   Crib biting and wind sucking – the horse grasps a fixed object between his teeth, arches his neck and swallows air. The eventual result is a distended gut and poor condition.

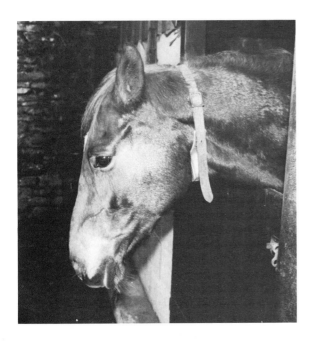

Fig 8   A gullet strap, fitted to prevent crib biting and wind sucking. The reason why horses indulge in this habit is unknown, but it seems to be related to stress and often occurs in horses with nervous dispositions. Often a change of life-style is the best means of discouraging the habit.

of the time, with the additional protection of a New Zealand rug and extra feed, but a shelter of some kind is necessary, if only for shoeing when it is wet, or for use should your horse be ill or injured and in need of nursing. More highly bred, thinner-skinned horses need better stabling and should be brought in at night in bad weather, and during the day in hot weather. All horses benefit from being turned out regularly, winter and summer and whenever they have a holiday, to graze, to be free to stretch their legs unencumbered by a rider, and to relax.

Apart from the horse's own accommodation, you need somewhere safe and dry to store his feed, bedding and other equipment. Having the right environment for your horse is half the secret of successful management.

THE PURCHASE

There are several ways of buying a horse: at an auction sale, through an agency, from a dealer, or privately. First-time buyers who have no previous experience of horses are often worried by tales of

13

unscrupulous sellers and dealers, and it is true that you might not end up with a good deal unless you have sought experienced help. There are all kinds of horses for sale: good, sound horses, with good conformation; sound horses with conformation faults which at best mean they won't have a chance in the show ring, and at worst that they will suffer some physical problem later in life; sound horses who may have behavioural or stable vices, or unreliable temperaments; and, finally, horses who are unsound in some way.

Unsoundness is not always immediately apparent, even to an experienced eye, which is why it is always advisable to have any horse vetted before you buy. If you are buying at auction, this is not possible and in this case you should have the horse vetted as soon as you get him home. At many horse sales auctioned horses are sold with a 48-hour warranty, which gives the purchaser an opportunity for redress if necessary.

The situation is further complicated by the fact

Fig 9   An anti-weaving grill. Weaving is another vice, associated with stress or boredom, in which the horse rhythmically waves his head from side to side and may actually rock from one forefoot to the other.

that some defects which are technically unsoundnesses may not necessarily render a horse unsuitable for a particular job. A vet will therefore report on the suitability of the horse for the use as described to him, for example as a hunter.

If a horse is sound and has no vices, it is unreasonable to expect a seller to point out conformation faults − it is up to the purchaser to decide whether the horse is capable of the performance that is required. Vices, whether stable vices such as weaving or behavioural vices such as rearing, ought to be pointed out, but an over-anxious seller might not do so. The purchaser ought therefore, to ensure that he buys the horse subject to him being free from any vices.

Buying Privately

There are advantages and disadvantages in all methods of buying horses. Most people feel safer buying from a private individual, and if you can buy a horse whom you already know, or on the recommendation of an experienced person whom you trust, so much the better. Unfortunately this is not always possible.

The disadvantage of buying privately is the time and expense involved − checking advertisements, making appointments and travelling long distances to see horses who frequently turn out to be unsuitable. When advertising a horse, the seller naturally wants to present him in the best possible light, so advertisements can be misleading, even unintentionally. The most frequently heard criticism of private advertisements is that the horse turns out to be somewhat smaller in the flesh than was claimed.

If you try to buy privately, the fact that you are only looking at one horse at a time, lacking any comparisons, may tempt you to believe that the horse you see is the one you want, even though he may not be quite what you originally had in mind. A keen seller might encourage you in this belief in order to conclude the sale of his horse.

Whilst it might not be a good idea for the first-time buyer to buy at auction, therefore, it would

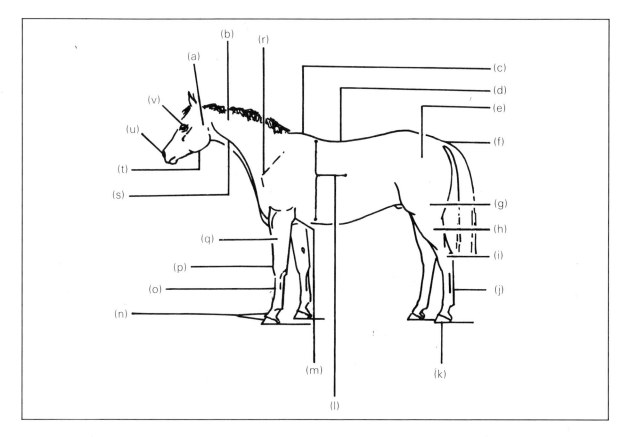

Key

(a) Head neat and in proportion, well set on to neck with room for flexion at throat and poll

(b) Neck long and graceful with no build-up of muscle on the underside

(c) Withers well defined, placing girth a hand's span behind elbow

(d) Strong, muscular back, neither too short nor too long

(e) Quarters rounded and muscular

(f) Tail well set on, neither too high nor too low

(g) Thighs well developed and muscular

(h) Second thigh well developed

(i) Hocks large, angular and well let down

(j) Back of cannon vertical and in line with buttock

(k) Hooves sound, symmetrical, each one the mirror of its opposite; hind feet slightly narrower than forefeet

(l) Deep girth and well sprung ribs allow plenty of room for heart and lungs

(m) Well-defined elbow with scope for movement

(n) Hoof/pastern axis approximately 45°

(o) Cannon short and straight with good dense bone

(p) Knee large and flat

(q) Forearm straight and muscular

(r) Sloping shoulder with scope for movement

(s) Well-defined jugular groove

(t) Width of fist between cheek-bones to allow plenty of room to breathe

(u) Muzzle neat with large nostrils

(v) Eyes bright, large and wide apart, with no white showing

Fig 10 Points of conformation. Note that the chest should be broad and the horse should stand square with 'one leg at each corner'; his legs should be straight and symmetrical viewed from front and rear.

be worth while visiting two or three sales, just to look at the horses, see what is available at what sort of prices, compare them with the type of horse you have in mind, learn as much as you can about conformation and try to get an 'eye for a horse'. Friends with horses, or your local riding school, can help in this respect. Be observant, mentally compare different types and breeds, and learn to recognise good and poor conformation. This time will not be wasted. Once you own a horse you will want him to perform as well as possible, and to look as well as possible. Understanding how your horse is made and how you can achieve improvements in both appearance and performance is part and parcel of good stable management, along with correct schooling and riding.

If you are making the effort to look at privately advertised horses, take an experienced person with you who will be able to point out obvious defects that you, with less experience, might miss, and who will be able to advise whether the horse is suitable for your needs. This is not an alternative to having the horse vetted − if you spare this expense you have only yourself to blame if things go wrong. It will, however, prevent you from making an obviously wrong choice: when you've made up your mind to buy a horse, the temptation is to do it quickly, but love at first sight is not the most reliable guide!

One advantage to buying privately is the possibility of having the horse on trial. Sellers may be reluctant to do this because of possible risk to the horse whilst it is out of their hands, but if the price is right, a mutually acceptable arrangement should be possible. Even without a trial, buying privately will allow you more time to assess a horse's suitability than you have at a sale. Don't be in a hurry. Ride and handle the horse until you are satisfied − in traffic, going away from home, in company and alone, and over fences if appropriate. Don't be put off making a thorough trial of the horse by a seller who presents him ready and tacked up, and expects a decision after five minutes riding around the home paddock. After all, you have probably travelled some distance to see the horse and will

be committing yourself to considerable expenditure should you decide to buy him. On the other hand, if the horse is obviously unsuitable, say so and don't waste the owner's time.

Auctions

If you buy a horse at an auction sale, it is unlikely that you will have the chance to ride him first. Horses will be on display in pens or stables before the sale and there may be an exercise area away from the auction ring, where some sellers will ride their horses prior to going into the ring. If you like the look of a particular horse you can always ask the owner to show it to you before the time comes for it to be sold. There will be a catalogue containing a description of each horse, where any vices or defects should also be stated. At most good sales horses must be entered with a 48-hour warranty by the seller. The way this usually operates is that the auctioneer holds the purchase monies for 48 hours after the sale, giving the buyer the opportunity to claim for breach of the warranty.

Conditions of sale at auctions may vary. It is therefore absolutely essential for any prospective purchaser to read the conditions of sale, which will be printed in the catalogue, and possibly displayed near the auction ring, very carefully. These conditions will indicate if warranties are given and will also state what they cover, for example, age, soundness in wind, limb and eye, freedom from vice, etc. Note that it is the seller who gives the warranty and is liable in the case of any breach, not the auctioneer. If there turns out to be a problem which could not have been detected within 48 hours, the buyer does not necessarily lose his right to redress, but the money will probably be more difficult to recover, the auctioneer by then having handed it over to the seller.

Agencies

Horse agencies are on the increase, particularly since computers have made it easy to maintain comprehensive lists of continuously updated

Fig 11   Penned horses at a sale. For the first-time buyer an auction sale can be a bewildering place.

information. These normally operate on the basis of a commission charged for putting sellers and buyers in touch with each other by way of a mailing list. Alternatively, there may be a registration fee instead of, or in addition to, a commission. Often, the seller only is charged. Agents obtain their customers through advertising and by word of mouth. When dealing with an agency it is important to realise that the sole function of the agency is to make introductions. The agency accepts no responsibility for what happens thereafter, nor for the accuracy of any description, nor the suitability of any horse, nor any other aspect of a sale. Any contract is purely between the buyer and seller. The advantage of an agency to a prospective buyer is the availability of a number of descriptions of horses for sale – how many depending upon the scope of the agency's operation.

Dealers

The fourth way of buying a horse is through a dealer, and these businessmen, in popular horse lore, probably have the worst reputation of all. It has to be said that horse dealers may be found in many different guises, from the competition horse buyer with literally hundreds of horses passing through his hands and operating on an international scale, right down to the gypsy or traveller, picking up ponies at country fairs. Frequently a dealer may be a breeder of horses or a competition rider in his own right. Bringing on young horses to sell is a way of meeting the expenses of competing for many riders. Another type of dealer is the one who buys horses going cheaply at horse sales and who may sell them wherever he can make a profit – to private homes for riding, or failing that, for slaughter.

The one advantage of buying from a dealer is that, for the sake of his reputation, upon which

17

his livelihood depends, he will usually take back
an unsuitable horse and replace it with another.
The terms upon which you buy from a dealer
should be similar to those agreed when buying
from a private individual. A good dealer will
often agree to a trial period, on appropriate terms.

The main disadvantage of buying from a dealer
is uncertainty about a horse's background and,
usually, a lack of registration papers of any kind.
The dealer's aim is to buy for little and sell for
much. Unless the horses he buys are unspoilt
youngsters (which the first-time buyer should not
be looking for anyway), there is usually a reason
why he has been able to buy them for relatively
little money. The reason may be straightforward,
or it may be that the horse has had problems
through being mishandled, or has been sold on
several occasions during his life and has never had
a chance to settle in one home. The buyer has no
way of knowing.

The dealer usually wants to move horses on
from his yard as quickly as possible, so any re-
schooling that has been carried out may have
been hurried, with short cuts possibly taken. If,
when you get your horse home, you find you have
problems, it is difficult to ascertain their cause
without knowing much about the horse's history.
Are you yourself the cause, through inexperi-
ence? Or has the horse's past experience led him
to behave in a particular way? An experienced
rider or horseman can tell much from a horse's
way of going, how he reacts to people generally
and how he behaves when handled, whereas the
first-time owner is often struggling in the dark.
The reasons why horses behave as they do, how
they should be handled for ease of management,
and how to build a rewarding relationship, will be
discussed in Chapter 8.

To summarise, when you view a horse with the

Fig 12   Always have a prospective purchase vetted
before you buy him.

intention of buying, ask yourself the following
questions:

1   Can I provide the right environment in which
to keep him?
2   Is he physically and mentally capable of what
I will ask of him?
3   Is he the right age for my requirements?
4   Is he the right size and type of horse for my
weight and build?
5   Is he sound? Have him vetted to be sure.
6   Is he free from vice?
7   Does he have any conformation defects and
are they likely to cause any trouble later?
8   What is his past history?

2 . Preparing for Horse Management

When the decision is taken to buy a horse, and the type of horse required decided upon, there are some other aspects of horse ownership to consider before the horse-box carrying the new acquisition turns in at your gate.

COSTS

The costs of owning a horse vary from place to place and from time to time, but one thing may be relied upon – the cost of the actual horse will by no means be the major part of the outlay. If you have grazing and stabling at home, the real cost of keeping a horse will be somewhat alleviated by not having to buy, rent or build accommodation specifically for him. Otherwise, the capital cost of buying land and a stable is likely to be considerably more than the amount you paid for the horse. Various ways of approaching the problem are possible. For example, you may have space at home in which to build a stable, or an outbuilding which can be converted. Grazing may be available to rent from a farmer within a reasonable distance from home. Whatever you decide, suitable arrangements must be made before the horse arrives.

The costs of horse keeping fall into two categories: initial (or capital) outlay, and recurring or running costs. The former includes the price of the horse and the cost of having him vetted; the capital expense of stable and field; tack such as saddle, bridle and their accessories, rugs and a headcollar; stable equipment such as feed bins, buckets, grooming kit and tools; your own riding clothes; and, possibly, a horse-box or trailer.

Running costs include items such as rent of stable or pasture; livery charges where applicable; feed and bedding; shoeing; vet's fees for routine visits and illnesses; insurance; membership of horse societies; entry fees; cost of diesel and lorry, truck or trailer maintenance; cost of pasture maintenance; and cost of riding lessons or riding permits.

Occasionally, there will be additonal items of equipment you wish to buy, or worn out or damaged items to replace. Of course, you can ride

Fig 13   Regular visits from the farrier are part of your running expenses.

19

with the minimum of basic equipment and facilities, at one extreme, whilst at the other there is no limit to the gadgetry and fancy tack which have been marketed to indulge the whims of horse owners. When budgeting for your horse keeping, work out what is essential for the basic welfare of the horse and begin from there. Co-ordinated travelling gear might look smart, but won't do you much good if you haven't first attended to your horse's general health and condition.

ACCOMMODATION

Where are you going to keep your horse, having bought him? Home might not necessarily be the most convenient choice. Apart from the need for proper facilities, looking after a horse is a seven day a week, twice a day (at least) commitment. What happens if, for example, you have to go away on business? Is there someone reliable who can look after your horse in your absence?

If you are working full time, livery might be a better choice for keeping your horse, leaving you free from worry when you are busy with other things, but giving you the advantage of having your own horse to ride at your own convenience. Several different kinds of livery service are available.

Firstly, full livery means that complete care of the horse will be provided in return for a fee. This usually entails a basic charge for stabling, bedding, feeding, watering and grooming, plus turning out for exercise as required. There is usually an additional fee if the horse is to be ridden for exercise (this is distinct from part livery, where the horse is used by the riding establishment where it is kept); further fees may cover turning out for shows, competitions or hunting, transport to and from events, and schooling by arrangement.

Part, or working, livery is often the arrangement when horses are liveried at an establishment run as a riding school as well as a livery yard. In this case, the horse is stabled and cared for in return for his use by the riding school,

Fig 14 Wherever you decide to keep your horse, remember he will appreciate company.

plus a reduced fee. It is worth noting that riding schools, that is establishments where horses are used for hire, must be licensed by the local authority. If you enter into such an arrangement, make sure that the establishment does have a licence.

Grass livery means that grazing, possibly, but not necessarily, with some form of shelter, and usually with supervision, will be provided in return for a fee. Supplementary feeding may be provided by arrangement.

Do-it-yourself livery means that the stabling facilities are provided for a fee, feed and bedding are usually available for purchase from the stable operator, but the owner attends to the care of the horse himself. This is a very useful option for owners who lack the facilities to keep a horse at home, but have the time available to care for him. When all is said and done, caring for your own horse is part of the joy of ownership.

In Britain a code of practice exists which is applicable to livery yards and, in fact, to anyone keeping horses. However, if you decide to keep your horse at a livery yard, it is a good idea to have the agreement set down in writing, stating what is to be provided for the fee before the commencement of the arrangement. There can then be no later dispute.

Arrangements between friends, for example to share rented accommodation and responsibility for attending to the horses, can often be convenient for all parties, but here again, mis-understandings can easily occur, or problems arise, when one party does not fulfil his part of the bargain. Therefore, as with livery arrangements, it is sensible to put all such agreements in writing, signed by all parties.

The same proviso applies to tenancy agreements when you rent stables or a field. Who is to be responsible for the maintenance of the stable? Whose job is it to keep the fences up and the pasture land in good heart? The landlord is usually responsible for maintenance of boundary fences, but if he fails to meet his obligations, you could find yourself liable should your horse escape and damage someone else's property. What happens if the landlord suddenly wants the land for his own use? How much notice must he give you, to enable you to find alternative accommodation? Similarly, how much notice must you give if you wish to move your horse elsewhere? It is best not to leave anything to chance, but to be absolutely clear on where you stand and what rights you have, when entering into any agreement with a third party concerning horses and the keeping of horses.

LEASING AND SHARED OWNERSHIP

Another situation that might arise when you first enter into the world of horse ownership is that of leasing or sharing a horse. Leasing is probably the simpler of the two to deal with. It is commonly used in respect of stallions standing at stud, but is also found in situations where an owner does not actually want to sell a horse and lose control over him, but has no further personal use for him. Such a horse may be, for example, a child's outgrown pony, or a horse whose competition days are over but who might still make a useful hunter or hack. The latter is often ideal for someone who has never previously owned a horse.

Matters a leasing agreement should cover include:

1. The length of the term of the lease.
2. The consideration, that is the price agreed.
3. The use to which the horse may be put and any exclusions.
4. Any requirements the lessor may have in respect of the well-being of the horse.
5. Any faults or defects the horse may have at the time of the lease.
6. What is to be done in case the horse suffers any injury or illness.
7. Provisions for insurance.
8. Provisions for any breaking of the agreement, or early termination of the lease by either party.

This is not an exhaustive list and either party may have additional matters they wish to cover, depending upon the individual circumstances.

Horse sharing is a little more complicated and may be fraught with difficulties unless an agreement is carefully worked out in advance. Matters which need to be covered include the responsibilities of each sharer regarding:

1. Ownership of the horse.
2. Daily care, buying feed and bedding.
3. Paying farriery and veterinary bills.
4. Providing grazing and stabling.
5. Providing and looking after tack and equipment.
6. Insurance.
7. The times at which each sharer may ride the horse.
8. The extent of the horse's activities (what happens when both sharers want to go to a different event on the same day, or on consecutive days? The horse must not be asked to

do the work of two horses, just because he has two riders).

9.   Arrangements for when one sharer is away on holiday.

Again, this is not an exhaustive list and each agreement must be worked out to suit the individual parties. The important thing is that nothing which may cause dissension later should be overlooked when the agreement is first worked out. It is easy to assume that you will get along with someone and not to bother with an agreement, but what seems reasonable to one person does not necessarily always seem reasonable to another. Situations change,and in cases of argument it is much easier to go back to a written agreement and check what you intended at the start.

INSURANCE

The question of insurance often causes difficulties. Many people, when they buy a horse, do not even consider the matter until it is drawn to their attention by chance. In Britain, horse insurance, unlike motor car insurance, is not compulsory. However, in the event of an accident, a horse owner may be liable in much the same way as a car driver. The extent of the damages which may be awarded to an injured party means that every horse owner should take out at least third party protection in the form of a public liability policy.

Your horse represents a considerable sum of money. Whether or not you insure him, however, may depend upon how you look at your investment, as the cost of insuring horses is comparatively high. A basic insurance policy will usually provide cover against the death of the horse due to accident, illness or disease. Comprehensive insurance packages may additionally cover theft or straying, permanent loss of use, personal accident to the rider, veterinary fees and loss of or damage to tack.

The golden rule is to read the small print and think carefully about what insurance cover you want to take out, then to check the policy details thoroughly to be sure that you are actually getting the cover you think you have paid for.

YOUR HORSE AND THE LAW

It is useful for the horse owner to be aware of the ways in which the law may relate to horses. In England, Wales and Scotland riding schools are controlled by the Riding Establishments Acts and inspections are made to see that standards are maintained.

The liabilities of private horse owners for the actions of their horses can be somewhat complicated. In general, horses must be fenced in and owners or keepers are responsible for any damage or expense caused by their animals straying on to the highway or on to someone else's land. Liability in other instances may depend upon matters such as whether a third party has suffered loss or damage as a result of the horse keeper's negligence; whether the keeper was aware that a horse might behave in a particularly dangerous manner and failed to give an appropriate warning; and whether the injured party was aware of the risks in a particular situation and was willing to accept them.

Riding on the public highway grows increasingly hazardous and it is essential, if you are going to ride on the road, to familiarise yourself with the Highway Code as it applies to riders, and to learn the rules of riding safely in traffic. Of course, you will want to get off the roads whenever possible, so it is also advisable to know the law relating to rights of way and bridle-ways, and any applicable local by-laws.

Finally, the Farriers' Registration Act, 1975, provides that only a registered farrier is legally permitted to shoe horses. Similar rules apply to veterinary surgeons, although many people treat horses for various problems, using so-called 'alternative' methods, without it being strictly legal to do so.

If you live outside Great Britain you should check how the law regarding horse ownership operates in your particular country or state.

3 . The Life Cycle of the Horse

Horses can live comfortably to around the age of 30. Some may even live up to 10 years longer. The majority of riding horses, however, are put down, due to injury, illness or the complications of both, at some point in their late teens or early twenties.

Horses may be ridden from the age of three until well into their twenties — some children's ponies play the role of schoolmaster to young beginners until they are 30 or more. From three to seven the horse is continuing to grow and mature, both physically and mentally. To give him the chance of a long and sound future career, he should be trained and worked progressively, and never asked to do more than that which is well within his present ability and level of training. This is the stage at which the horse who is overfaced becomes afraid to jump and the horse who is jumped too often becomes sour and starts to refuse. Whether you are doing dressage, endurance riding or racing, work your young horse too hard too soon and soundness problems will occur.

From eight to twelve, a comparatively short period of his life, the horse is considered to be at his competitive peak (if you can find a good eight-year-old offered for sale, don't expect him to be cheap!). Fortunately many horses who have been cared for competently go on competing for much longer. For event horses the limit is usually around 15, while endurance horses, showjumpers and dressage horses may go on for another two or three years. Horses can be found hunting and doing riding club work up to about 24 years old, and a horse can go on hacking as long as he is physically comfortable carrying a rider.

What do you do with your horse when you can no longer ride him? This is something you should think about *before* you become involved in horse ownership. There are only two responsible choices: to retire the horse, in which case you must make sure he is happy and well cared for to the end of his natural life span, or to have him quietly put down. Later in this chapter the problems of caring for aged horses, and what happens when euthanasia is decided upon, will be discussed.

What must the owner do to reap the rewards of good management and ensure the horse's welfare through the various stages of his life?

BREEDING

At some point during years of involvement with horses, you will inevitably experience a desire to breed your own horse. If you embark on this course, there are many good books on the subject to help you with the technical aspects (*see* Further Reading). From the point of view of horse management, the question is, should you breed from your mare and, if you do, have you the commitment it takes to raise a young horse successfully?

'Fools breed horses for wise men to ride' is a saying with more than a ring of truth for the private horse owner. If you think you can sell the youngster and make a profit, forget it — you will be very lucky to recoup most of your costs. Add to that the difficulty of choosing the right sire, the risk to your mare, and the element of chance that makes the result of your breeding experiment uncertain (even when it looks right on paper) and the prospect of breeding your own horse might not look so attractive. Throw in the cost and time involved in raising the foal to maturity and the inevitable accidents which afflict the lively, curious young horse, and you might wonder why anyone breeds horses at all. That said, there can be few experiences more rewarding than watching your home-bred foal mature into a healthy, well-mannered adult horse who is a pleasure to ride.

Consider your mare carefully before you decide to breed. She should be healthy, in good condition, and sound. Owners are often tempted to breed from mares who have been retired prematurely from competition due to unsoundness. If the unsoundness is due entirely to accidental injury, there is no problem, but if there is any likelihood that it could be hereditary, it would be unwise to breed from such a mare. Also think about the type of horse you are planning to breed and the use you have in mind for it as an adult. You might well be able to breed yourself a competition horse by using a Thoroughbred stallion on a half-bred mare, but if your mare is obviously the wrong type for what you want, save

yourself time and money and buy a new horse instead.

The private horse owner should never indulge the desire to breed unless the future of the offspring is pre-planned. Too many young horses, bewildered and unwanted, still end up in the sale ring and, subsequently, the abattoir.

THE YOUNG HORSE

When your mare produces a foal, the major part of your breeding experiment is just beginning. Ahead lie three years of care and attention before you can think about getting on the youngster's back. It is not just a question of waiting until the foal is old enough and big enough to ride — those three years can be put to good use in giving your youngster a basic education. This should include being taught to lead in hand from either side, being groomed, learning to stand quietly whilst

Fig 15   The home-bred foal.

Fig 16   Basic education begins at an early age for this Shetland foal in a sea of legs at his first show.

being attended to in the stable, and having his feet picked up and trimmed. He can also be mouthed, with a special mouthing bit which has keys attached to the mouthpiece for him to play with until he gets used to the idea. This will be useful when the time comes to back him; colts, especially, may need to be led from a bridle rather than a headcollar as they become bigger and stronger.

Although your young horse is not being ridden and worked, his health and well-being require as much attention as that of an older horse. He must be fed properly while he is growing and developing to maintain healthy condition, neither too fat (as many young show horses unfortunately often are), nor too thin. He should be vaccinated against tetanus and influenza, and his teeth should be checked regularly: twice a year between the ages of two and five when new teeth are erupting. It is particularly important that the young horse should have his feet trimmed regularly. If his feet are not correctly balanced,

the uneven distribution of weight over his joints can cause abnormal development and limb deformities. A regular worming programme will help prevent a build-up of these parasites which can cause damage to the internal organs, unthriftiness, colic and other illnesses.

Towards the end of his three-year-old summer the young horse can be backed and lightly ridden for a few weeks before being turned away for the winter. If his early training has been kind and thorough, this stage should present no problems. The term 'breaking in' is often used to describe this stage of a horse's life, but is accurately applicable only to the youngster who has lived a virtually untouched 'herd' existence until the age of three, in which case the whole job is much harder.

Whenever force is used, the result is never as successful as when the horse is trained by kindness and gentle repetitive conditioning. A horse who is forced to submit to his handler will be resentful and unco-operative, rather than a willing and happy companion. In handling your horse, however, 'force' should not be confused with 'firmness'. Treat your horse firmly but kindly and force should never come into the equation. 'Training' is a better word than 'breaking in' to describe the whole of the horse's education, including the part where he learns what it means to be ridden. The trainer should, of course, be a competent person who understands the technique of developing the horse's physique to carry a rider, of teaching him to accept the bit and to respond to the aids, so if you do not have enough experience to undertake the task yourself, get some professional help. Teaching the horse correctly from the start will save many problems later on.

In the spring when he reaches the age of four, the young horse should be ready to be ridden on lightly, mainly doing basic schooling and hacking out. He may do a few shows or, towards the end of the summer, two or three small showjumping competitions, if he is destined for competition work. Your management should be geared

Fig 17 Competence, kindness and firmness have all been employed in giving this young Haflinger stallion his basic training.

towards helping him stay fit and healthy, and enjoying his work. He will possibly not have spent a great deal of time in the stable until this stage of his career, so this is a good time to consolidate early training and make sure good stable manners are established.

Ideally, the four-year-old will be turned away for the winter again, to rest and grow until the following spring. Turning him away does not mean forgetting about him – he still needs all his regular care and attention.

THE COMPETING HORSE

At five the horse's career will become more specialised, according to the direction you intend to take. Is he a showjumper, eventer, or an endurance or dressage prospect? Perhaps you are thinking of hunting or showing (he may already have been shown in-hand as a youngster), or perhaps you simply want him to be a competent all-rounder and pleasure horse.

From now on the management of your horse, including his ridden training, will be primarily determined by the career which you are planning for him. His success will depend as much upon good management as on good riding. As he grows older, the horse's physique, abilities and fitness levels change according to the work he is doing, and the work he has done in the past. The good manager will be aware of this and will be able to make adjustments to the horse's routine, feed and management methods to take account of his condition and help him to work to the best of his ability.

RETIREMENT

With good management and a measure of luck, you will have many years of pleasure, fun and good riding with your horse. Eventually the day must come, however, when the serious working stage of his life comes to an end. You decide to 'retire' him to an easier way of life, but what exactly does this mean?

Fig 18   At the age of five, the young horse can be ridden on and further training can begin.

Fig 19   Well cared for, your horse or pony will reward you with years of pleasure.

The image is conjured up of a sunny meadow with good grass and a gently flowing stream, with your horse peacefully and contentedly grazing, swishing his tail occasionally to flick away a troublesome fly.

There is a bit more to it than that. Just as the young horse needs daily attention before he is old enough to be ridden, the aged horse needs an equal amount of care to ensure his comfort and well-being. When a horse has been used to regular exercise all his life, plus the fun and excitement of competition work, it is not kind suddenly to stop riding him altogether, and worse to put him in a field on his own, or with unsuitable company, and leave him to his own devices.

When you decide to retire your horse from hard work, let him down gradually, to give his body systems time to adapt. Provided he is still fit and healthy, go on riding him − he will enjoy regular

27

Fig 20   When he can no longer work so hard, you must decide what to do for the remaining years of the horse's life.

hacking, or the odd day or half day hunting for quite a few more years. If you haven't the time or don't want to be bothered with doing this yourself, find someone who will enjoy the opportunity of quietly riding him out.

It may be possible to find a good home for him through his later years. If you do this, check out his new home thoroughly and reassure yourself that your horse really will be looked after. All kinds of arrangements are possible, such as lending or leasing the horse, or selling him at a low figure, whilst retaining the option to have him back. If you have owned a horse throughout his working life, you owe it to him to see that he is well treated during his old age and is put down painlessly when the time comes.

In retirement, in addition to routine care, such as having his feet trimmed and being wormed regularly, the aged horse may need extra attention to his teeth and diet, and to his warmth and comfort when the weather is cold. For example, he may need different or specially prepared food which is more easily chewed and digested. Although horses are gregarious animals and are unhappy alone, choose his companions, and how they are managed, carefully. An older horse often makes a good companion for a lively youngster; provided he is not infirm, he will establish his seniority and help the younger horse to settle down. However, if he is getting too old and slow, too lively a companion could worry him and cause problems at feeding time, when the aged horse needs time and peace to eat and digest his meal.

EUTHANASIA

Of course, however well you care for your horse, the end has to come eventually. You may go out one morning and find your aged horse has simply died in the night, but it is more likely that you will have to make the decision to put him down. Letting someone else make that decision by sending the horse to market before this stage is finally reached is not an option worthy of consideration, although it happens to many unfortunate aged horses. Like the unwanted youngsters previously mentioned, they end up herded together in the back of the meat man's lorry. No true horseman would ever allow his old companion to come to such an end.

Horses may be put down by your veterinary surgeon, at an abattoir, by the local 'knacker', or by someone authorised from your local hunt kennels. Carcass value is highest if the horse is sent to an abattoir, and if you make enquiries the operator will explain the exact procedure to you. Check if your horse is likely to be kept waiting once he arrives and, if so, what the facilities are for caring for him until his turn comes. Of course, if the horse is suffering from some disease or has

been treated with certain drugs, the carcass value will be reduced.

Most caring owners, in any case, prefer their horses to be put down at home, in familiar surroundings, so that the whole business is over before the horse has any inkling of what is happening. The usual procedure is to lead the horse out and offer him a bucket containing some favourite food. When he lowers his head the vet will immediately shoot him through the skull with a humane killer. Death is instantaneous, although reflex movements may occur for a short while afterwards.

An alternative method of putting the horse down is by injection, with an overdose of anaesthetic, although this method is less frequently used and the carcass is valueless.

It is sad to lose an old friend, but if you have looked after your horse well during his life, you will have many happy memories and the knowledge that you did your best for him, including doing the right thing at the end.

4 . Stabling

What is a stable? The word can conjure up pictures of anything from a top-class establishment, representing an investment of millions of pounds or dollars, to a makeshift galvanised iron and timber shed. The former is really the application of modern horse technology at its highest level, undoubtedly incorporating the latest veterinary and other therapeutic facilities, along with a high standard of buildings, provisions for schooling, training, breeding, or whatever the speciality of the establishment demands. The latter, however, may be a shelter at need, but is certainly not a stable in terms of the basic requirements of a well cared for riding horse.

The purpose of a stable is to provide a shelter in which the horse has enough room to turn around, lie down, roll and get up comfortably. It must be warm in winter but not too warm in summer, airy and well ventilated but not draughty, and dry and properly drained. The arrangements of the stable itself and its ancillary buildings should provide the horse owner with a convenient means of caring for his horse in the traditions of good horse management. What kind of buildings serve this purpose and how should you set about building, converting or modernising your own stable?

TRADITIONAL STABLES

Apart from minor details, technology has not been able to improve much on the basic design of the traditional stable block, which, if well built, whether of stone, brick or other local materials, fulfilled all the requirements mentioned above. The cheapness of labour in the past meant that convenience might not have been taken into account when arranging for the storage of hay and straw, or the disposal of manure, while the practice of putting the hay-loft above the boxes

constitutes an unacceptable fire risk today. However, provided sensible adaptations are made to take today's safety, labour-saving and hygiene requirements into account, traditional buildings can still provide some of the best equine accommodation possible.

Traditional stables are frequently found built around a central courtyard, a system which is both convenient and practical, provided the manure heap is not situated in the middle, as was sometimes the case. The arrangement provides a sheltered aspect to the open sides of all the boxes and gives the horses the benefit of visible company across the yard, whilst the comings and goings of horses and people keep them alert and interested in their surroundings, preventing boredom. There is also a clear enclosed space where horses can be led out, run up, mounted and dismounted.

The buildings themselves usually have the advantage of thick, solid walls, combined with slate or tiled roofs, keeping them relatively warm in winter and cool in summer. Many modern materials do not provide sufficient insulation in winter, nor reflection against the heat of the sun in summer. This is one reason why galvanised iron is particularly unsuitable for stable construction. Traditionally constructed stables are usually sound and solid, provided proper maintenance has been carried out, and will stand up well to the more robust effects of equine occupation, such as kicking, banging and chewing. As they were built in an age when the horse was still the main means of transportation and pulling power, and his needs were therefore widely and thoroughly understood, practical details, such as the avoidance of any projections or sharp edges, the most suitable positioning of mangers, hay-racks and tie rings, and the use of the most durable materials available, were incorporated into the design as a matter of course.

Fig 21 Often used to construct field shelters, galvanised iron is not suitable for stables that are constantly in use.

The disadvantages of traditional purpose-built stabling have come to be recognised as scientific understanding of the horse improves, but can usually be resolved fairly easily. For example, a single building would contain loose boxes, connected by an internal passageway, often with a hay-store above, which was reached by a narrow stair or ladder. To allow for the hay-store, ceilings to the boxes would be low. Windows, usually rather small, would be provided in the front wall of the passageway, or at either end, as much to allow in some natural light as to provide through ventilation.

Today, we know that dust and mould spores from hay and straw are the working horse's worst enemy, but the type of stabling described can easily be improved to avoid the problem, by storing hay and straw elsewhere, raising the ceiling height of the loose boxes and improving the ventilation. The natural ventilation system can be improved by means of air inlets at low level, with outlets in the roof or high in the walls.

The outlets can be simple hoppers, or suitably designed windows, fanlights or rooflights which will also give additional natural light. Alternatively, a mechanical ventilation system can be installed.

Floor construction can be a problem in renovating older stables if the original has worn down badly, cracked, broken up, or has gaps between floor bricks, for example, where stale urine can be trapped. Your stable floor needs to be hard-wearing, non-slip, non-absorbent, smooth and of the minimum fall necessary to maintain efficient drainage.

Traditional stables, updated to meet modern needs, also have the advantage that it is quite an easy matter to make them look attractive, an important consideration in areas where statutory planning requirements apply.

PLANNING NEW STABLES

Most horse owners, however, will not have the advantage of purpose-built traditional stables in which to keep their horses, and a choice will have to be made regarding the best means of providing stabling within the owner's budget. There may be the possibility of converting an existing building, such as a barn or cowshed, into stabling. Otherwise, it will be a case of starting from scratch and building new stables. Whatever the choice, some basic aspects of planning should be considered before you start digging the foundations.

Few private horse owners will want more than six or eight loose boxes, with ancillary accommodation such as tack and feed rooms, whereas, once likely costs are considered, the single horse owner will find it as economic to build two boxes with an adjoining tack room/store as to build a single loose box. After all, there is always the possibility that a second horse will one day arrive on the scene, perhaps a pony for a child, or a younger replacement for an ageing companion. In any case, horses do like company and if you can keep two horses, rather than just one, so much the better.

STABLE TYPES

Field Shelters

The absolute minimum you are likely to require is a simple field shelter. This is intended to provide shelter from bad weather in winter and from heat and flies in summer. It can, if necessary, be used as a stable when, for example, a horse is sick, or needs special care, or for tacking up and grooming in inclement weather. It should, however, be soundly constructed, of durable materials and, for the reasons previously mentioned, galvanised iron is not a suitable cladding. The design is usually for a rectangular building of, say, 14ft x 12ft (4m 20cm x 3m 60cm), with half of one long side left open. It is practical to fit a door to the opening so that the shelter can be closed if

required. If possible, a concrete base, or at least some form of hard, compacted floor, should be provided, or the ground inside the shelter will become wet and muddy and will greatly reduce the usefulness of the building.

American Barn Systems

An alternative form of stabling is the American barn system, which comprises one large-frame building with partitioned loose boxes constructed inside, leaving a central walkway. The size of the barn can vary to accommodate any number of horses from about four up to the sizes required by large commercial establishments. The advantage is that it puts the whole stable routine under cover. The disadvantage is that it creates an increasingly artificial environment and particular care has to be taken with the ventilation system to prevent respiratory problems and the spread of infections possibly faster than would be the case with traditional stabling. Hay and straw should not be stored in the area where horses are stabled, both to prevent a dusty environment and the risk of fire.

The barn system is unlikely to be an economic proposition for the pleasure horse owner, unless you have an existing barn into which loose boxes, either of permanent construction, or of the prefabricated, demountable type, can be incorporated.

STABLE CONSTRUCTION

Siting

The information below assumes that you have grazing adjoining or close by your house, with room to build a small range of boxes and ancillary stores.

For the sake of convenience, you will want your stables close to the house, but not so close or in such a position that smells, drainage run-off, or even bits of hay and straw will pollute the domestic environment. In this respect, the slope of the ground and the direction of the prevailing

Fig 22   Barn stabling in Kentucky.

wind must be taken into account. A level site for your stables is best, but is not always available, and a certain amount of excavation may be necessary to obtain the best position.

The open sides of the boxes, that is the side containing the door openings, should be protected from cold north or east winds, which may not be the same as the prevailing wind. If the buildings themselves do not provide sufficient protection, it will be necessary to consider an alternative wind-break, for example trees. Sometimes the natural lie of the ground will provide shelter, but do not build your stables in a hollow that gets little sunlight, catches the frost, and retains a damp atmosphere. Also avoid exposed hilltops.

The ground conditions of the site must be assessed and, if necessary, land drains put in to ensure adequate drainage of the site, away from the new stables and the existing house.

A further point to remember when planning the siting of your stables is accessibility, not only for your own horse-box or trailer, but also for delivery trucks bringing hay and straw, or removing manure. The length of any drive or access road and the distance over which it is necessary to run essential services (electricity and water supplies) will have a considerable bearing on the total cost.

Specialist Services

It is obvious from a simple consideration of the essential aspects of siting that there is more to building stables than getting together with a few friends and throwing up some concrete blocks. If

33

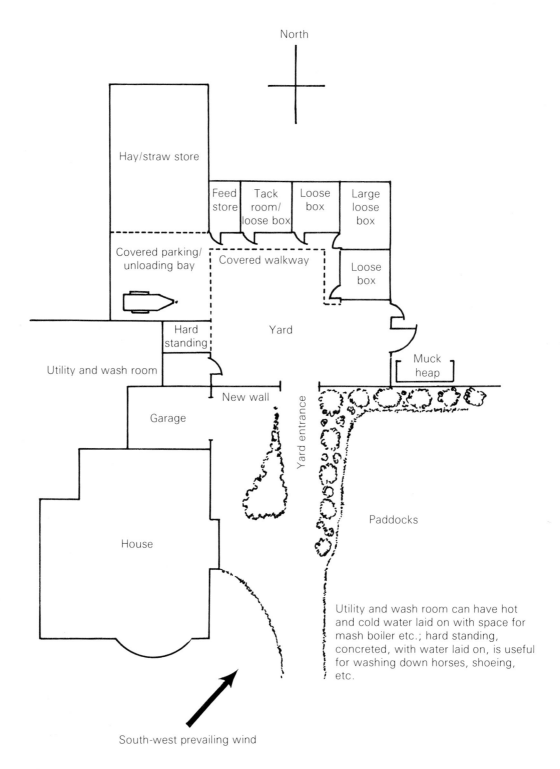

North

Hay/straw store

Feed store

Tack room/loose box

Loose box

Large loose box

Covered parking/unloading bay

Covered walkway

Loose box

Hard standing

Yard

Utility and wash room

Muck heap

New wall

Garage

Yard entrance

House

Paddocks

Utility and wash room can have hot and cold water laid on with space for mash boiler etc.; hard standing, concreted, with water laid on, is useful for washing down horses, shoeing, etc.

South-west prevailing wind

Fig 23   A possible layout for a new stable yard.

you are aware of building requirements and you know enough about horses to know what you want and need, there is no reason why do-it-yourself stabling should not be a success. However, if you don't understand building construction, or are new to horse ownership, you could save yourself a good deal of trouble and expense by calling in the experts. There are several ways of doing this, depending upon the type of stabling you want.

Many people nowadays find the simplest answer is to opt for one of the many prefabricated stable designs on the market. The superstructure of such buildings is usually timber and it is up to you to organise your own site preparation and put in foundations. However, companies that supply this type of stabling invariably also offer a design service and will advise on all essential preparation and groundwork. At a price, a complete service is usually available, from discussion of the basic siting and design, to the supply of the last tie ring or bucket holder. However, the actual laying of drains and construction of footings will usually have to be carried out by your own builder.

If you want more substantial buildings of block or stone, built in traditional style, you will almost certainly need to employ an architect — but be sure that the architect understands the special requirements of stable buildings. To get an idea of what you should build, look at other owners' stables and consider their advantages and drawbacks. Major points to consider include the safety of the horse and his manager, fire risk, convenience, provision of a healthy environment for the horse, avoiding conflict with adjoining land uses and accessibility of motor traffic to the stables and of the horse to riding areas.

Statutory Requirements

Before you build anything, check the legal requirements for planning or building permission, or any other statutory regulations of a general or local nature that might apply. In Britain, with minor exceptions, planning permission from the local planning authority is required for all new buildings. If you employ an architect, he should be able to advise on all such matters as part of his service.

Layout and Design

The type of construction you choose will depend, among other things, upon cost, time available for building, location, availability of materials, and personal preference. The next thing to consider is the actual layout and design of the buildings.

The simplest layout for a range of two boxes with a tack room/feed store is a straight line; if more boxes are required, an L-shaped layout may be preferred. Fire precautions should be taken into account when designing a bulk store for hay and straw in conjunction with stables, and in the overall layout, choice of materials and the electrical installation.

The most practical size of construction for loose boxes is 12ft x 12ft (3m 60cm x 3m 60cm), which will accommodate most riding horses comfortably. A generous size is 14ft x 12ft (4m 20cm x 3m 60cm), whilst 12ft x 10ft (3m 60cm x 3m) is adequate for average horses. Ponies can be accommodated in boxes of 10ft x 10ft (3m x 3m). It makes sense to opt for the largest size you can afford, however, as a sick horse or a foaling mare will need more space, and larger stables will allow for any change in your future needs.

Doors are traditonally in two leaves, so that the top half can be left open for ventilation and to allow the horse to look out. They should open outwards and catches should be provided so that they can be fastened back to the wall when open. Strong closing bolts should be fitted, of the padlock or autolock type, and a kick-over bolt is usually fitted at the bottom of the door for convenience. Windows should be designed not to project into the stables when open, and glass should be protected by means of metal grilles.

A fresh, clean water supply is essential and, if possible, hot and cold should be laid on. The usual method of watering horses is to use buckets, but automatic drinking supplies are a possible alternative, although they have the disadvantages of requiring regular maintenance and making it impossible to tell how much a horse

Fig 24   This purpose-designed stabling has a central walkway and a hay store at the far end. It is in a high, exposed area and the interior is insulated for more warmth.

Fig 25   A safety clip has been attached to the door bolt to foil this escapologist.

is drinking. Water supply pipes must be protected against freezing up – nothing is worse than finding your stable water supply out of action in the depths of winter.

The electricity supply also requires knowledgeable installation. All supply cables must be protected from damage by horses, preferably by chasing them into the walls and by avoiding running cables through boxes where they are accessible to the occupants. Power points and switches should be installed outside the boxes, usually on the front wall, and light fittings should be of the bulkhead type, at high level. The electrical installation should be waterproof and light fittings should not be placed where they will be in close proximity to stored hay and straw.

Mangers and hay-racks may be built in, or prefabricated fittings can be used. The important thing is that they should be strong, securely fixed, and free of any dangerous projections. Suitable wall or corner racks, bucket holders, and support frames for removable polythene or galvanised mangers are purpose-designed, practical and easily available from various suppliers. Tie rings, and those for attaching hay-nets, must be securely fixed so as not to come away from the wall should the horse pull back on them.

The positioning of all these fittings is a matter of comfort for the horse and convenience and safety for the manager. Water buckets should be placed away from mangers, to discourage horses from drinking and eating at the same time. Some owners like to place mangers and hay-nets on the wall opposite the door, or in the far corner, others on the wall inside the door. Traditionally, the tie ring is on the far wall, near the hay-rack or hay-net ring. Tie rings and hay-net rings should be about 5ft 6in high (1m 65cm), so that the empty hay-net, when correctly fixed, will not hang too low, with the risk that the horse's feet may become entangled in it.

If you are building no more than two loose boxes, you will probably want to combine your feed store and tack room. Again, a wide choice of proprietary fittings is availabe, for storing both tack and feed. Shop around and choose what best meets your needs. Feed may be stored in anything from galvanised steel bins to plastic dustbins. The important thing is to see that the containers are watertight and vermin-proof. Shelves will be needed to store smaller items, and possibly a cupboard for medicines and first aid equipment.

If you plan to cook linseed or barley, a boiler or other means of cooking will be required, but it is not a good idea to have this in the same room as your tack – steam from the boiler will create a damp atmosphere, in which leather may be attacked by mildew and will be liable to rot.

Saddles should be stored individually on saddle horses to keep their shape and prevent damage. Bridles, girths, martingales, bits and other tack can be hung on appropriately spaced hooks, whilst a trunk and boxes, or deep shelves, will be needed to store rugs and bandages. A sink will be required for washing and cleaning tack and other equipment, preferably with hot and cold water laid on. In view of the amount of time you are likely to spend in your tack room, and the need to keep tack dry and aired, some form of heating, such as a wall-mounted fan heater, is advisable. With water in constant use, electric radiant fires are unsafe.

When designing your stables, consider how your daily routine can be made convenient, with the minimum of hard work involved. Keep the trip to the muck-heap as short as possible, but site the muck-heap downwind of your house and stables and, if possible, at a lower level. Make adequate drainage arrangements, whether to a main sewer or to a soak-away into a field, and construct the muck-heap so that the contents can be squared off and kept within the allotted space, without becoming spread around your stable yard.

When building a range of stables of the type described, it is practical to provide a deep overhang with a concreted walkway at the front, to provide protection from the weather and a hard surface that can be swept clean in front of the boxes. Support posts to the overhang should be avoided, as they are an unnecessary obstruction in front of the stables.

Hay and straw stores should be as well ventilated as possible, leaving a clear space around the stacked bales, including keeping them

Fig 26 Modern, purpose-built, timber stabling with a concreted walkway and a deep overhang for shelter.

off the floor by means of sleepers, open pallets or some other system allowing for through ventilation. Stacking bales off the floor also helps discourage rats and mice.

Fire precautions, taken into account in the construction of your stables, should also include the provision of adequate fire extinguishers, suitably positioned, with clear instructions for use. Where staff are employed to look after horses, or where several people are involved, a fire drill notice should be prominently displayed. Smoking should be banned in feed and forage stores and loose boxes, and generally discouraged in the stable yard.

Security

A final point to consider, although not a pleasant one, is stable security. Thefts from stables left unattended at night, especially those separate from a dwelling, are an increasing problem, not only thefts of horses, but of tack and other valuable equipment. There are various precautions that can be taken, from fitting secure locks and bars to windows, to floodlighting and comprehensive burglar alarm systems. Guard dogs can be very effective in deterring thieves, whilst locking devices are available to prevent the theft of trailers and other movable equipment. How far you go in this respect is up to you, but don't leave your stables unprotected.

5 . Grazing and Pasture Management

You now have a horse, and have provided a stable that meets all the requirements mentioned in Chapter 4 — so why do you need a field at all?

The most fundamental reason is that the closer we can keep a horse to his natural environment, the healthier and happier he is. Of course, the horse's health and happiness form only part of his relationship with his owner or manager: competition horses are required to perform at a level which no horse in its natural state could achieve; working horses, such as dray horses or police horses in towns, have to be kept stabled for long periods without turn-out facilities in order to do their jobs. However, competition riders recognise the benefits of turning out their horses, even for a couple of hours a day, while the sight of brewery dray horses kicking up their heels on their annual 'holiday' leaves no room for doubt that they appreciate the break and the chance to follow their natural behaviour patterns.

The horse, a naturally sociable creature, has lent himself easily to domestication, but he still retains the instinct and habits of his own, independent species. The more natural the environment we can provide, within the limitations of the work we require the horse to do, the better his health and temperament will be, and the easier he will be to manage.

Food, water and shelter are the three basic requirements of the horse in his natural environment. Searching for these also ensures that the wild horse gets enough exercise to remain healthy. The domesticated horse is protected from many of the dangers that threaten the wild horse: predators, many risks of injury and disease that may lead to illness or an unpleasant death, and, we hope, from shortage of food, water and shelter that might result in starvation, dehydration and exposure, also followed by death.

The basic needs of the horse and how they are affected by his domestication, will be considered more fully in Chapter 6. Here, we will concentrate on how best to utilise our available pasture to fulfil the horse's needs of food, water, shelter and exercise.

Fig 27   All horses benefit from being turned out for a few hours each day.

FOOD

How much pasture does a horse need? In the wild the habitat of a herd of horses may be described in miles or kilometres rather than acres or hectares and the herd will move seasonally, following the availability of grazing. In the domestic situation, horses are usually kept in much smaller groups and measures can be taken to see that the grazing provided is of sufficient quality to meet the horses' nutritional needs. On this basis, one acre (0.4 hectares) to one horse or pony is usually adequate for summer grazing. However, this only applies where the pasture is well managed and if the horse is to live out or, in particular, to winter out, then two acres (0.8 hectares) per horse should be considered the minimum required.

WATER

A clean, fresh water supply is as essential to the horse as enough nutritional food, so if you want to be saved the trouble of carrying endless buckets, a field with a good natural water supply, or with mains water laid on, is a major advantage. A good natural supply can be provided by a free-flowing stream, deep enough that the horse does not suck up grit or sand whilst drinking, which can cause sand colic, and flowing quickly enough to avoid the water becoming stagnant. Small streams and water ditches must be cleared regularly to ensure an adequate supply and it is important to check that the stream is not polluted from some source further upstream. Natural springs provide a good and usually pure source of water, but again a sufficiently deep drinking spot is needed. Pond water, unless a natural spring is its source, soon becomes stagnant, flat and unpalatable, and is not a suitable supply.

Where mains water is connected, drinking troughs must be provided. Ideally they are set back into the fence line, to avoid any low edges projecting into the field on which the horse might knock himself. Troughs should preferably be purpose-built and on no account should containers which might have sharp edges or dangerous protrusions (for example, an old bath), be used instead. Troughs must be regularly cleaned out to prevent the accumulation of dead leaves, algae, sediment from the water and other rubbish. The supply system, usually an enclosed ballcock, must also be checked regularly to make sure that it is operating freely.

Carrying water to a field by hand is a hard chore and not to be recommended, when you consider that the average horse consumes about 10 to 12 gallons (45.5 to 54.6 litres) per day. Since the capacity of most buckets is about three gallons (13.6 litres), this means carrying three or four buckets of water to the field each day for each horse. Few horse owners have the time or energy for such a task.

During winter, water supplies often freeze over and it is necessary to break the ice two or three times a day, to enable the horse to drink. Mains water supply pipes should be protected against frost.

SHELTER

The third essential requirement of the horse at grass is shelter. For the sake of convenience of management this may include a field shelter of the type described in Chapter 4, and in the absence of natural shelter, some sort of constructed protection is essential. Horses need shelter from wind and driving rain or snow in winter and from the heat of the sun and flies in summer. Other man-made shelters include an open-ended covered shed, supported on strong uprights, or even more simply designed angled screens (see Figs 28 and 29). The latter give protection from the wind more than from anything else.

However, horses tend to prefer natural shelter whenever possible, which is why frustrated owners often see their horses cowering under a hedge in the rain rather than making use of the expensively provided field shelter where they could stay dry and warm.

Natural shelter depends on the topography and slope of the land, the direction of the prevailing

Fig 28 A simple field shelter.

Fig 29 A three-sided wind-break, useful when ponies are kept in a field where there is little shelter. Such a wind-break needs to be firmly constructed.

wind and the wind that brings the worst winter weather, ususally north or east. It may be provided by natural vegetation in the form of trees or hedges and sometimes by other natural phenomena such as cliffs or rock formations. For example, moorland ponies can often be found sheltering under the large rocky outcrops of tors at the summits of windswept hills. A fold or hollow in the ground will also provide shelter and you may notice that your horse has a favourite spot in the field where he will often lie down.

In winter your horse will choose different places to stand, according to the weather of the day, the wind direction and the shelter he needs. On very windy days he may well avoid standing under the same tree that affords him shade from the sun and flies in summer.

The survival of the horse in the wild frequently depended upon his ability to flee from predators, so he has a highly developed awareness of the need to stay alert to danger and be able to see what is going on around him at all times. This is the reason that horses avoid enclosed spaces, such as the field shelter previously mentioned. It also explains why a horse, particularly one that is alone in a field, will often stay in the most open or exposed area of pasture, rather than seeking more shelter near a hedge. Unless the weather is very bad, he will simply turn his tail to the wind and wait, head down, for conditions to improve. Similarly, in summer, when he wants to doze, he will choose the same open area.

TURNING OUT

Many owners do not ride their horses during the working week, but turn them out 'for exercise'. This applies to horses kept at livery as much as to those kept privately at home. The horse kept on 'maintenance' rations will get as much exercise as he needs in moving around the field to graze, with an occasional brief fling to stretch his legs when he feels so inclined. However, if you can only ride

Fig 30 Sheltering from the sun and flies.

your horse at weekends, do not expect to keep him competition fit by filling him up with oats then turning him out into a small paddock to 'exercise' himself. One acre (0.4 hectares), for example, gives a fit horse very little scope for athletic activity and if he has also been made over exuberant by too much food and too little real work, turning him out is asking for trouble — in terms of damage to himself, to other horses who may share the grazing with him and to the property itself. (A combination of overfeeding and insufficient exercise is also dangerous to the horse's health.)

Therefore, unless you have unlimited space and do not require your horse to be fit for anything more than hacking, or the occasional show or riding club competition, turning out is no substitute for ridden work, or even lungeing or longreining. The benefits of turning out are seen more in the horse's mental state than in his physical fitness. It gives him a chance to relax and, if possible, to enjoy the company of his own kind, in a situation as close to his natural environment as possible.

SAFETY

Having looked at what the horse needs from his field, there are one or two practical matters to consider before discussing pasture management in greater detail.

Fencing

The field must be secure enough to prevent the horse from escaping and, it is to be hoped, to prevent anyone from trying to steal him. It must also provide a safe environment. The choice of fencing is affected by both these considerations. Probably the best secure boundary is a well-maintained, cut and laid hedge, being strong and secure, whilst providing a good degree of shelter and being difficult, if not impossible, to remove.

Fig 31 Loose and sagging wire — a recipe for disaster.

Such hedges are rare in today's automated world, requiring skilled and labour-intensive maintenance. Many hedges that do exist have fallen into disrepair, the breached areas often having been 'repaired' with strands of barbed wire or sheets of unsightly galvanised iron, which frequently cause serious injuries to horses. Plain wire can be equally dangerous if not properly strained — never leave horses in a field fenced with sagging wire of any kind.

The traditionally favoured fencing for horse paddocks is post and rail, preferably of seasoned oak. This is expensive (even without using seasoned oak!), and therefore may not be a practical choice for the private horse owner. Post and wire is a frequently used alternative, but these fences require regular maintenance and the wire must be kept taut. Nowadays, there are various forms of proprietary fencing available, for example those based on heavy-duty, plastic-covered wire, which can be attached to timber uprights to form a safe and durable fence.

Boundary fences need to be secure against possible horse thieves, unpleasant though the necessity may be, whilst gates should be strong, secure and lockable. Reversing the top hinge, so that the gate cannot be easily lifted off, is a good idea. Heavy-duty chains and strong padlocks are an advisable precaution.

Field Hazards

Many horses are kept on the edge of urban areas and even in rural surroundings, the dumping of rubbish into fields can be a problem. All kinds of dangerous objects may be tossed over hedges, from polythene bags to tin cans and glass bottles. Before turning your horse out into a new field, and as a regular precaution, check it for dangerous objects and rubbish that might be lying around. Even on farms, lengths of wire, or parts from machines, can be accidentally or carelessly left lying in fields and become hidden in the grass.

PASTURE MANAGEMENT

The ideal horse pasture provides a good mixture of palatable and nutritive grasses and herbs, kept in good heart and free from poisonous plants and weeds. This cannot be achieved without some attention to regular management. Even pasture that starts off in good condition rapidly becomes sour if grazed solely and continuously by horses. Horses are selective eaters, which means that they pick and choose which plants they prefer, leaving those not to their taste to grow out of control. They will not eat in the same areas where they dung, so the grass in these areas soon becomes rank and overgrown. If the pasture is not rested periodically, and is stocked to the limit, the good grass will soon be eaten down to the ground, leaving space for weeds, such as docks and thistles, to take over. Finally, the worm burden of paddocks used solely for horses increases, as there is no break introduced into the life cycle of the parasites. The more heavily the land is grazed, the more opportunity the worms have to multiply.

Good Pasture Preparation

The first requirement of grazing land for horses is that it should be well drained. Badly drained land will become severely poached if stocked in winter and foot problems occur if horses' feet become soft through continually standing on wet ground. If your land is wet, seek expert advice on the laying of land drains.

The quality of pasture is affected by the type of soil on which it grows, which may be acid or alkaline and may vary from light and sandy to heavy clay. A sandy soil may be too dry to grow good grass, but organic farmyard manure will both fertilise the soil and help improve moisture retention. Heavy clay soil becomes badly poached in winter and drainage may be essential. The most productive and easily managed soil is a sandy loam, combining the best of both extremes, without the disadvantages. To produce good grass, soil needs to be slightly acidic. If it is too acid, weeds will grow at the expense of the grass, and if too alkaline, the soil will not release the

Fig 32   When pasture is grazed to the limit, the weeds take over. Here are thistles, docks and buttercups.

nutrients needed for good grass growth. If you are unsure of the condition of your soil and unhappy with its productivity, it is a good idea to have the soil analysed. Alkaline soils can be improved by a dressing of farmyard manure, whilst acid soils should be limed.

Horse pasture is usually permanent pasture, that is land that is used continuously as grazing land and is not ploughed up nor rotated into other uses. Permanent pasture, which has not been ploughed for many years, if ever, contains a good mixture of herbage and grasses, but along with the most palatable and nutritious grasses is likely to be an assortment of less valuable grasses and weeds. Provided the land is kept in good heart and the weeds kept under control, this will not be a problem, as horses do not need lush grazing, whereas they will benefit from the nutrients available in a wide selection of plants.

Pasture which has been regularly reseeded, sometimes including rotation into other uses, is termed 'ley' and is usually laid up for hay or silage making. It is less suitable than permanent pasture for grazing horses, as the grass mixtures used tend to produce rich grazing with a high nitrogen content.

As a pleasure horse owner you will probably be concerned only with a relatively small area of permanent pasture, which you will want to keep in good condition. The main difficulty with managing small areas of grassland is that it is not worth buying all the machinery needed for the work. The best thing to do, for those jobs too onerous to do by hand, is to persuade a neighbouring farmer to lend or hire you his equipment, or to do the job for you, if he can spare the time.

Good Pasture Maintenance

Each pasture maintenance task should be carried out at the appropriate time of year to obtain the

45

Fig 33 Field grasses (left to right): perennial rye-grass, timothy, fescue, cocks foot, all found in good pastureland; slender foxtail of poor quality; oat grass, found in hedgerows; sweet vernal, common in meadows and sweet smelling, but unpalatable; Yorkshire fog, a common, tufted grass of poor nutritional value.

greatest benefit, beginning at the end of winter or very early spring with harrowing. The purpose of harrowing is to remove dead vegetation, allowing air and fertilisers to reach the soil and leaving room for the new growth.

Reseeding, if necessary, should be done after harrowing, or it can be done in the autumn. Use a mixture recommended for your area — advice may be sought from seed merchants and local government advisers. The basic ingredient in good pasture is perennial rye-grass, other ingredients including timothy, cocksfoot, fescue and clover. Too much clover should not be encouraged in horse pasture as it provides rich grazing, which may lead to digestive problems or laminitis in susceptible horses.

The next task is to roll the pasture to get rid of divots and poached areas and firm up reseeded land. Rolling must be done before the ground becomes dry and hard, but not whilst it is still wet and sticky. Rolling is especially important to provide a good surface if you want to ride in the field.

To promote grass growth, fertilisation of the soil is necessary, the main nutrients required being lime (for calcium), nitrogen, phosphate and potash. Unless situated in a limestone region horse pasture is likely to require liming occasionally to maintain the correct acidity (pH value) of the soil. Liming should be carried out in early spring before the new growth starts.

Nitrogen, phosphate and potash can be applied together as a compound chemical fertiliser in the spring and again during the summer as paddocks are rested. Soil analysis will give you the right ratios of each to use. Nitrogen is easily washed out of the soil, so is only used during the growing season. Animals must be kept off newly fertilised

Fig 34 Ragwort — a poisonous weed, more dangerous when wilted than when growing. Ragwort should be pulled by hand and burned.

pasture until the chemicals have been washed well into the ground, as the pellets could cause colic or poisoning if swallowed. Alternatively, there are various organic fertilisers available which are growing in popularity, especially with owners of breeding stock. Farmyard manure is probably the most frequently used organic fertiliser and can be spread in the spring or autumn. Ideally it will be well broken down when spread and the weather will finish the job.

If you cannot put cattle or sheep on your pasture to clear the areas rejected by your horse, it is a good idea to mow the grass two or three times during the summer. This will discourage weeds and promote a good 'bottom' to the grazing. Always cart away or burn the clippings as they can be dangerous to horses when wilted.

Poisonous plants are one of the major dangers in horse pasture and a constant watch must be kept to see that they do not get a chance to establish themselves. The most common and dangerous of these is ragwort. It should be pulled by hand and burned. The growing plant is usually left alone by horses but it becomes more palatable when wilted and can be very dangerous if it gets

Fig 35 Laburnum — this poisonous tree has distinctive yellow flowers, which have progressed into seed-pods here.

into hay. Spraying will deal with most other plants and weeds, such as docks, thistles and buttercups and a simple knapsack sprayer is ideal for controlling weeds in small areas. Bracken may cause poisoning, usually where grazing is poor in the late summer and autumn.

Some trees are unsuitable for hedging as they may be poisonous to horses and it is advisable to check before planting new boundary hedges or wind-breaks. Yew is the most deadly tree found in Britain and privet, laburnum, laurel and rhododendron are also poisonous. Horses will seldom eat poisonous plants, unless the grazing is very sparse, many of them tasting bitter and unpalatable, so the answer is to keep your grazing in good heart and control the weeds.

As already mentioned, combined grazing with sheep and cattle is an excellent method of management. The sheep and cattle will eat the grass and plants left behind by horses and will help to fertilise the pasture naturally, whilst also reducing the horse parasite burden of the land — most parasites cannot be passed between species. Worm eggs can survive cold weather but may die if exposed to hot sun, so harrowing to break up the droppings in summer, if you do not remove them from the pasture, will help kill off the eggs.

Finally, hedging and ditching need to be carried out during the winter months. Hedges must be trimmed to prevent trees growing too tall and their roots breaking up the hedge bottom, gaps must be repaired, wire fences checked and the wire tightened where necessary. Ditches must be cleared to maintain efficient drainage and to prevent silting up and the blocking of water supplies.

6 . Daily Horse Care

In the previous chapters, the basic needs of the horse have been discussed in terms firstly of survival, secondly of staying healthy in an artificial environment, that is, a domesticated environment, and thirdly of the facilities necessary for horse keeping and the possibilities of livery.

ESTABLISHING A ROUTINE

Wherever your horse is kept, some sort of routine will have to be established to ensure that his daily needs are met and that nothing important is omitted. A livery yard or riding school will have its own daily timetable and staff rota system, so that everyone knows what to do and when to do it. If your horse is kept at a commerical establishment, you will have to fit in with the basic arrangements of the yard. Keeping your horse at home will give you more flexibility in your organisation, but your horse will always need attention at least twice a day, even when turned away at grass.

There are basically three recognised methods of horse keeping: stabled, at grass or the combined system. The last means stabling the horse part of the time and turning him out for the remainder; usually he is stabled at night in winter then turned out during the day in a New Zealand rug, whilst in summer he is turned out at night and brought in away from flies during the day.

The method you choose will depend upon the extent of the grazing available, the age, breed and type of horse, and the use you want to make of him. There is a very good case for turning horses out as much as possible, if not all the time, but many horse owners do not have sufficient pasture to be able to do this. For practical purposes, we will consider a suitable routine for an adult riding horse kept by the combined method summer and winter. As many owners acquire their first horse in the spring, looking forward to the better weather, we will begin at the point where the winter rugs are coming off, the horse is slipping his winter coat and the first flush of new grass is coming through.

THE COMBINED SYSTEM

The lorry drives into your yard, down comes the ramp and your horse is led out — from now on he is your responsibility. You have a field and a stable ready and waiting, but where do you put him first? When do you feed him? What should he have? Is there anything else you ought to do when your horse first arrives?

When you buy a horse, it is a good idea to find out as much as you can about how he has been kept in the past. Has he been kept out or in? What diet is he used to? Is he a 'good doer'? Does he eat up well or is he picky about his food? How much hay is he used to and is it fed soaked or dry? What bedding does he have? Is he usually rugged at night? What about during the winter? And is his vaccination certificate up to date?

Once your horse arrives, put him in his stable where you can keep an eye on him after his journey and where he can settle down and get used to his new home. If he has had to travel more than a short distance, he may be thirsty, so offer him a drink. If possible, it is best to have water freely available to your horse at all times. Give him a hay-net and, having removed his travelling clothes and made sure he is none the worse for his journey (check him over quickly for any minor injuries) leave him to rest.

Most horses will settle quickly in an airy, dry and comfortable stable, but let your new horse relax for at least a couple of hours before offering him his hard feed. Control of equine parasites is

Fig 36   Removing the headcollar, with the horse turned towards the gate.

based on minimising their spread, so it is a good idea to worm any new horse on arrival, then keep him off his new pasture for 48 hours, while the dose takes effect. The final important thing to do is to ensure that your horse has been vaccinated against tetanus — never take the risk of your horse catching this horribly distressing disease.

When you are ready to turn your horse out, lead him into his field and turn him to face the gate while you close it. Talk to him quietly and stroke his neck before removing his headcollar or lead rope. Many horses are inclined to pull away as soon as they get through a field gate and this should be firmly but quietly discouraged. To begin with, you may wish to leave your horse with his headcollar on, until you become accustomed to catching him easily. In this case, use a leather headcollar, which will break if it becomes caught up in a hedge or fence, not a nylon one. Make sure that it fits well, not so tightly that it rubs the horse's face or restricts his jaw, but securely enough not to be easily shaken off.

If you are keeping your horse by the combined system, you will often find that during the spring and autumn the weather is kind enough to leave him out night and day; horses, on the whole, would rather be out than in. If he has been used to a night rug in the stable and a New Zealand during the day all winter, remove them gradually as spring progresses. First, on warm days, discard the New Zealand and when he is used to being out all day without a rug, choose a warm spell in which to leave off the night rug. If he is now staying out at night, you can take the New Zealand off during the day and replace it at night, for a few days.

Check what kind of pasture your horse has been accustomed to in the past. If you have good grazing and he has only had an hour or two a day on poor grass, as often happens, don't turn him out for too long at first, as too much rich grass, too suddenly, could cause colic. A few days should be sufficient to accustom him to the change.

Keeping your horse by the combined system

entails far less work in summer, when he can be out most of the time, than in winter, when you will have to muck out every morning. In Britain you will rarely have to bring your horse in out of the heat during the day, especially if there are some trees in his field to provide shade. However, this may be necessary in hotter climates, especially when the sun is fiercest around midday. Towards the end of the summer and early autumn, flies may be a nuisance and you will easily be able to tell if they are bothering your horse as he will stand shaking his head and swishing his tail. Horses out together stand nose to tail to flick the flies from each other's faces. Various fly repellents, both sprays and long-lasting tie-on tags, are available. Their efficiency varies and you may find that one of them helps discourage flies from pestering your horse.

The main problem you are likely to encounter by turning your horse out in good grazing in early summer, is that he will put on more weight than you might wish if you are planning to compete. In this case, you must decide by observation how much time he needs to spend off the pasture. Horses can, in fact, work off grass, provided you set out slowly. However, the best plan is probably to bring your horse in some time before you want to ride him, especially if you want to do any fast work.

Summer: Daily Routine

Assuming you are at work during the day, your daily summer routine might look something like this:

7.30 a.m. Prepare feed and take to horse in field. Check horse over in field and check water supply. Notice whether horse behaves as normal; if not, why not?
8.30 a.m. Go to work.
6.00 p.m. Return home. Bring horse into stable and groom him.
6.30 p.m. Have tea.
7.00 p.m. Ride.
8.00 p.m. Return and groom horse. Check for injuries.

8.30 p.m. Turn horse out and feed in field, allowing him to drink first.

Winter: Daily Routine

In winter your timetable will be rather different. Many people find it impossible to ride during the week in winter and restrict their activities to weekends, but if you are hunting, or training for long distance rides early in the season, your horse must be exercised, either early in the morning or when you get home at night. Riding on the roads after dark is not to be recommended, but if you have to do it, make sure that you can see and be seen by wearing a fluorescent safety device, such as a belt or tabard, plus boots for your horse and stirrup lights, white in front and red behind. If you do not ride your horse during the week, he must be turned out for exercise and even if you do ride him, he will benefit from being turned out during the day, if you have sufficient land available without your grazing becoming poached and muddy. Your routine might be as follows:

Fig 37 A reflective light for riding after dark.

6.30 a.m. Muck out stable and groom horse.

7.00 a.m. Ride.

8.00 a.m. Return from ride. Groom horse and replace rugs. Water and feed horse. Refill hay-net or turn horse out in New Zealand rug and hang hay-net in suitable place in field.

8.30 a.m. Go to work.

6.00 p.m. Return home. Bring horse in. Groom and ride if you did not ride in the morning. Otherwise change New Zealand rug for night rug (and blankets if horse is clipped), checking horse over as you go. Pick out feet. Lay down bed. Water and feed horse. Refill hay-net.

10.00 p.m. Final check on horse. Final feed if appropriate. Refill hay-net if needed.

Having sketched out your basic daily routine winter and summer, we will now consider what needs to be done in more detail.

FEEDING

In the wild, the horse eats continuously, grazing whilst on the move and refilling his comparatively small stomach, but never overloading it with too much at one time. A horse who is kept out will be seen intermittently grazing and resting, following his natural instinct. To work, your horse needs additional food, both bulk food for roughage and concentrates for energy and body-building. These may be in the form of hay, plus either grain or compound proprietary feed respectively. Even if he is not doing much work he will need extra feed in winter to keep him in good condition.

It is better for the horse's digestive system, therefore, if you can feed him little and often — fit competition horses are frequently fed four or five times a day. However, provided a horse is out at grass, or has hay to munch on whilst stabled, it is adequate to feed him twice a day, morning and evening, if your commitments make it difficult to feed him more often.

If a horse is receiving four or five feeds a day, they obviously need to be given at fairly regular intervals, with the largest feed given last thing at night. However, if you are feeding only twice a day, you can be a little more flexible about feeding times, to suit your convenience, provided the feeds are spaced well apart. Traditionally, a fixed routine should be adhered to, but since this is necessarily upset whenever a horse has to travel to a competition, there may be some merit in varying feeding times to a certain extent. The important thing is that the horse should have a balanced diet, the quantities varying only because of changes in his work-load or condition, and not because it is too much trouble to go out and feed him.

Varieties and quantities of feed will be considered in Chapter 7, but basically you should feed your horse according to his type, size, temperament and the work he is expected to do. The more work he does, the more energy-giving concentrates he will need. Always cut down the concentrates (hard feed) if the horse is off work for any reason; otherwise, when the horse is brought back into work, there is a risk of azoturia, or 'tying up' (see Chapter 15). If hard feed is cut down, the bulk feed should be correspondingly increased.

Any changes in the diet must be made gradually, over several days, as the horse's rather complicated digestive system needs time to adapt.

The quality of food fed to horses is very important and should be the best you can buy. Poor quality food may be rejected, or may cause digestive problems if eaten. Dusty or mouldy hay, in particular, will adversely affect performance and may cause respiratory problems.

The horse cannot digest his dinner efficiently and work hard at the same time, so always exercise your horse first, then give him a short time to relax and cool off before feeding. Also avoid fast work immediately after your horse has had a drink. It is considered preferable for the horse to drink before feeding rather than after, so if your horse does not have water freely available, offer him a drink before his feed.

BEDDING AND MUCKING OUT

There are several types of bedding which are acceptable and safe for horses, the most commonly used being straw. Good quality long oat straw is preferred, and it won't hurt a horse who is partial to nibbling it, although eating the bedding should be discouraged. There are few sights as attractive as a comfortably stabled horse lying in a thick bed of golden oat straw in a softly lit stable on a winter's evening. Unfortunately, good straw, whether oat, wheat or barley, is hard to come by, the most readily available being short length, combine harvested straw. Short straw is less easy to manage, even when of good quality. Dusty or mouldy straw provides a bed that invites respiratory trouble, especially if the horse is inclined to eat it, as many do.

The most commonly used alternative to straw is wood shavings, which can make an economical and easy to manage bedding. These are available pre-packed, and some firms will also supply them 'dust-free', or you can buy them even more cheaply from timber merchants, either bagged or loose. In the latter case you must be careful to see that no wood chunks or splinters, or other dangerous objects such as nails, have found their way into the wood shavings.

For a really hygienic, dust-free bedding, shredded paper is increasing in popularity. It can also be bought pre-packed. Shredded paper is very absorbent, and you must be careful to remove all wet bedding when mucking out, to avoid strong ammonia fumes from the urine lingering in the stable.

Another option is moss peat, which is available in some areas and, if carefully managed, will provide a safe, warm bedding.

A good bed in your stable provides the horse with a warm, clean and comfortable place to lie down. It provides easier standing, preventing strain on the legs, helps prevent draughts, encourages the horse to stale (urinate) when he needs to and helps prevent injury when he is getting up or lying down.

To provide all these things efficiently, the bed

Fig 38   Hygienic shredded paper bedding.

must be mucked out and relaid every day when the stable is in use. The method for a straw bed is as follows:

1. Tie the horse up or turn him out.
2. Remove water buckets and hay-net for refilling.
3. Remove droppings and soiled straw, piling clean straw in one corner of the stable. Be very careful to keep the prongs of your fork, if you use one, away from the horse if he is in the stable — nasty accidents can occur if a suddenly startled horse jumps on to the prongs of a stable fork.
4. Put the wet and soiled straw straight into a skip or wheelbarrow placed just outside the stable door, for removal when you have finished the job. It is not a good idea to leave the horse tied up unattended in the stable, especially with the door open. A tied up horse may panic if startled and struggle to get free, possibly injuring himself, or breaking his headcollar in the process.
5. Sweep the stable floor clean and, if the horse is to be left in, re-lay the straw as a thinner day bed. If the horse is going out, the floor can be left clear to dry and the bed re-laid later.

With a bed of wood shavings, the droppings should be removed and the shavings tossed against the sides of the box to be aerated. Any loose droppings will separate from the shavings and can be removed — the easiest and quickest way is by hand with a pair of gloves kept for the purpose. Any completely soaked shavings should be removed; the remainder will dry out and can be spread again later. Toss all the bedding from one side of the box against the opposite wall one day and reverse the process the following day. This will avoid stale bedding being left in the corners.

Paper bedding can be treated in much the same way as wood shavings. With peat bedding the wet peat and droppings should be removed, loose droppings raked out and the peat thrown against the sides of the box to be aerated for a short time before being re-laid.

Your horse's bed should be thick enough to prevent his feet from going through to the stable floor, and the bedding should be banked up around the sides of the box to prevent draughts and help avoid injury when he is getting up or lying down.

The deep litter method is theoretically a labour-saving way of providing bedding. It consists of laying a deep initial bed, removing the droppings each day and adding fresh straw, shavings or peat, without disturbing the existing bed. The whole bed is then periodically removed and thrown away, approximately every three months. This requires extremely good management and the stable must be very well drained if you are to avoid smells and a wet surface which can lead to foot problems in your horse. It does save time in mucking out every day, but is hard work when the whole bed has to be removed, unless you have mechanical means of doing so.

When you have finished mucking out, refill the water buckets and hay-net and attend to your horse as necessary. Buckets, mangers and other feeding utensils should be rinsed clean after use.

GROOMING

Your horse needs to be groomed for several reasons, the obvious ones being to remove mud and dirt so that you can tack him up and ride him, and to improve his appearance. Other reasons are: to maintain his skin and coat in a healthy condition, and thus help prevent skin diseases by assisting in the removal of waste products and stimulating the circulation of the blood; to improve muscle tone by 'strapping' and 'banging'; to get the horse used to being handled; and as a means of checking him over every day for injuries.

'Quartering' is the name given to the initial grooming of the day, when you give your horse a quick brush over and pick out his feet before exercise. 'Strapping' is the thorough grooming a stabled horse should have, preferably after exercise, when he is warm and his circulation is working faster. This really cleans his coat thoroughly and improves his muscle tone. A

Fig 39   Grooming, using the body brush and curry comb.

horse kept at grass should not be strapped, as he needs the natural oils and a certain amount of dust in his coat to keep warm. Similarly, he should not be bathed, except for special occasions, when care must be taken to see that he does not catch a chill. Correct methods of grooming and how to turn your horse out smartly are discussed in Chapter 12.

Apart from your daily routine, there are several other matters which need attention on a regular basis (see Figs 48 and 49).

FOOT CARE

Many owners neglect their horses' feet, mainly through not realising the importance of regular skilled attention and not understanding what is required.

In comparison to his weight, the horse's feet are tiny, all his weight being transmitted to the ground through four small points. When this is understood, it is easy to appreciate the tremendous stresses and strains borne in the feet and legs, both when the horse is stationary and, more importantly, when he is moving. If his feet are not trimmed and shod so as to be evenly balanced, the pressure on his limbs will not only be heavy, but abnormal. The results of this can be found in all kinds of joint and limb conditions, caused either by sudden injury due to imbalance, or by the progressive effects of abnormal stress. In many cases permanent damage may be caused.

The problem is that these conditions often do not noticeably inconvenience the horse until it is too late to do anything about them, whereas if the owner had understood the principles of good shoeing, the damage might never have occurred.

Horses' feet vary in shape, depending upon breed and type. Basically, however, when a horse is standing straight and square on a level surface, the hoof-pastern axis (that is, a line drawn straight through the pastern and hoof to the ground) must be parallel with the front of the hoof

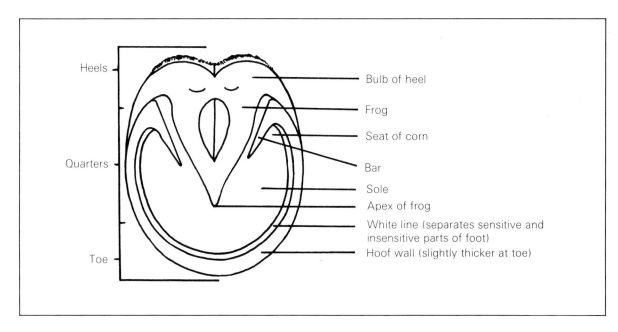

Heels

Quarters

Toe

Bulb of heel

Frog

Seat of corn

Bar

Sole

Apex of frog

White line (separates sensitive and insensitive parts of foot)

Hoof wall (slightly thicker at toe)

Fig 40 The ground surface of the foot.

Fig 41 Fitting a horseshoe is a skilled task.

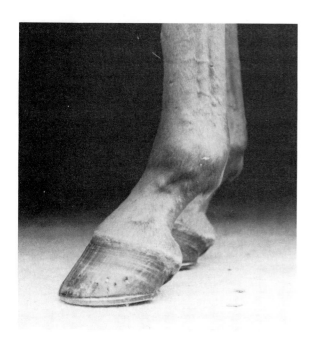

Fig 42 A well-shod forefoot. This horse has road studs fitted and you can see how the foot is immediately unbalanced on a completely level surface (see Chapter 11).

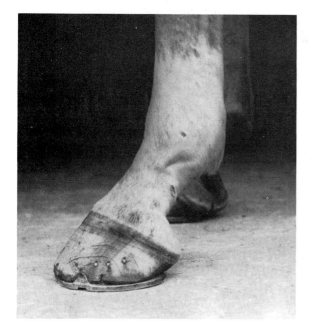

Fig 43 A well-shod hind foot. The heels have been left sufficiently long to give support.

wall, when viewed from the side. From the front, the hoof/pastern axis should be a vertical line, through the centre of the fetlock joint, the pastern and the hoof, ending at the toe. Some horses may have either pigeon-toed or splay-footed conformation and careful shoeing can help to compensate for these defects.

Horses' feet grow at varying rates, but in general the feet need attention from the farrier every four to six weeks if the horse is shod and working, or every four to six weeks when the horse is unshod. Young horses should have their feet trimmed regularly from an early age, to ensure correct and level growth, both of the feet and limbs. There is little point in complaining to your farrier about the state of your horse's feet if you only call him out once every three months.

PARASITES

All horses carry worms, and the aim of good management is to minimise their effect and prevent their spread. The most dangerous of these parasites are large and small strongyles. These two groups of strongyles have differing life cycles and affect the horse in different ways. The large strongyle larvae are swallowed by the horse whilst he is grazing, then migrate through the system from the intestines, causing damage to the blood vessel walls. They finally return to the intestines where they mature and lay eggs, which are expelled by the horse in the faeces to start the cycle over again. The whole process takes from six to nine months.

The small strongyles spend their lives in the gut. The larvae burrow into the intestinal wall, where they mature, before emerging again to continue their life cycle to the egg-laying stage. The problem occurs in the spring, when large numbers of larvae pass from the intestinal walls into the gut, causing diarrhoea and loss of weight.

Other internal parasites which affect horses are: ascarids, which mainly affect young horses, causing unthriftiness, digestive upsets and sometimes also respiratory problems; lungworms, which rarely infect horses but can cause coughing

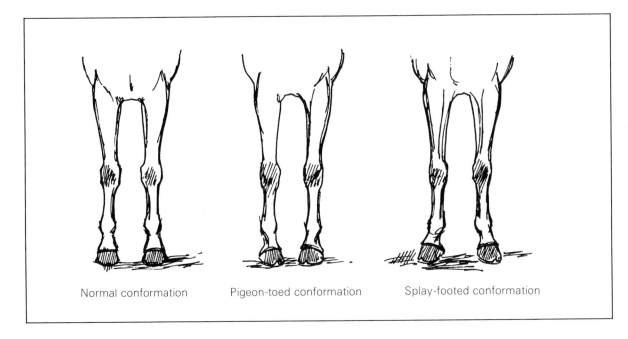

Normal conformation   Pigeon-toed conformation   Splay-footed conformation

Fig 44 Conformation of the feet.

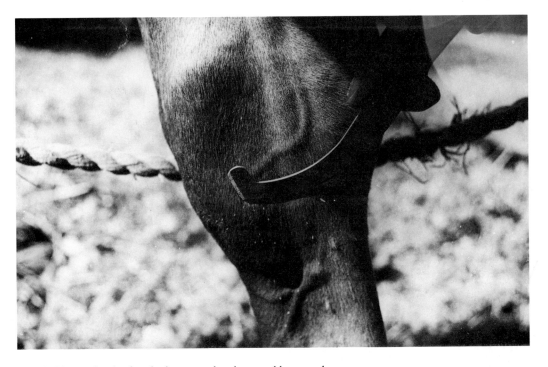

Fig 45 Using a bot knife, which is curved and serrated but not sharp, to remove
the tiny yellow eggs which the bot fly lays on the horse's coat.

and lung damage; and bots, the larval stage of the bot fly, which attach themselves to the stomach lining, where they may cause problems. Bot flies pester horses in the late summer, when they lay their easily recognisable yellow eggs on the horse's coat, usually around the legs, where the horse will rub or lick them off and swallow them. Scraping off the eggs with a bot knife or similar implement helps prevent infestation.

Treatment

There are many worming preparations on the market, incorporating various 'families' of drugs. Parasites may build up a resistance to one particular family if it is used without variation, so change to a different type of drug every so often to avoid this happening. Many preparations will kill only adult worms, although some, such as those containing ivermectin, will deal with the larvae, including bots, and will help guard against some external parasites. Choose your wormer carefully, making sure it will do the job required. In general, horses continually grazing the same pasture, in company with other horses, should be wormed every six to eight weeks, more often in summer,

Fig 46 Giving a paste wormer by syringe.

when the worm activity is greatest. If you have only one horse and plenty of grazing, you can worm him less frequently.

Anthelmintics, the drugs used to combat parasitic worms, are available in various forms, as powders or granules to be added to the horse's feed, or as a paste in a ready-to-use syringe. Many horses refuse to eat food that has had a wormer mixed with it, so the syringe form is usually the surest and easiest method of dosing your horse. Slip one hand over the horse's nose and, with the other, slide the syringe into the side of his mouth, between the teeth; depress the plunger so that the paste, which is sticky, is deposited on the tongue. Most wormers have been made to taste palatable and few horses object if you do the job calmly and quietly.

Wormers can also be given by your vet by stomach tube, if it is necessary to be sure that a full dose is given, for example, if a horse has a seriously debilitating worm burden. This is not usually necessary, however, since worming is one aspect of routine health care that the owner can easily deal with himself.

Prevention

Picking up the droppings in your pasture every day, or harrowing the field in summer to spread the droppings, so that the sun can kill the eggs, will help reduce the worm burden. Putting cattle or sheep in your horse pasture will also help, as horse parasites do not affect them and they will help clear the ground. Otherwise, worm eggs can survive undisturbed in the ground for many months and any pasture grazed continually by horses will never be completely free of them.

VETERINARY CHECKS

Two routine jobs will have to be done each year by your veterinary surgeon: checking your horse's teeth and giving him his vaccinations against influenza and tetanus.

Teeth

The constant use of the horse's cheek teeth, or molars, to grind his food results in wear of the surface. Fortunately the horse's teeth continue to grow throughout his life, which allows for this wear. However, the upper jaw is wider than the lower jaw and this, together with the motion that the horse employs in masticating his food, results in uneven wear, leaving sharp edges on the outside of the upper teeth and the inside of the lower teeth. These sharp edges can cut the inside of the cheek, or cause discomfort with the bit and, in extreme cases, difficulty in eating. The teeth therefore need regular attention to remove the sharp edges by rasping them level. The process is painless and should be carried out at least once a year. Checks should be made twice a year on horses between the ages of two and five, when their permanent teeth are erupting, and on aged horses, who may have difficulty with eating.

Vaccinations

Tetanus, or lockjaw, is one of the most agonising diseases that can affect horses, both for the horse and for the owner who has to watch its slow progress, knowing there is little chance of recovery. When you buy a horse, if there is no proof that the horse has been vaccinated – he should have a certificate giving the information – ask your vet to deal with the matter immediately. After the initial injections, a month or so apart, a booster should be given twelve months later and then, on the advice of your vet, probably every two to three years.

The second vaccination your horse will need is for protection against equine influenza. This is a

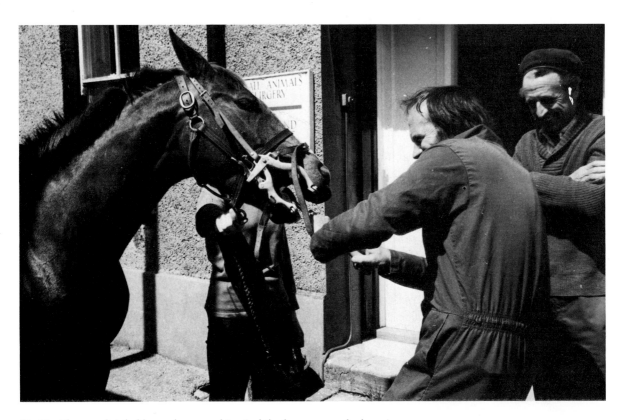

Fig 47 The mouth is held open by a metal 'gag' while the vet rasps the horse's teeth.

	WEEK 1	WEEK 2	WEEK 3	WEEK 4
Jan	Continue hedging, fencing and ditching			Worm, including bots
Feb	Bring in horse to start training; check teeth; feet trimmed and shod	Horse can be trace clipped if he has not started to slip his winter coat	Harrow pasture	
Mar	Re-seed pasture if required; lime & fertilise		Re-shoe; end of basic fitness training, subject to weather conditions	Roll pasture, weather and ground conditions permitting
Apr.				Re-shoe; worm; clean and store winter rugs when out of use
May	Rasp teeth if necessary	Fertilize resting pasture; pull and spray weeds		Worm; mow pasture in use to discourage weeds; remove clippings from pasture and burn
June	Harrow pasture during hot weather to disperse worm eggs / Re-shoe			Mow pasture
July	Worm		Re-shoe / Hay-making ⟵ ———— ⟶	
Aug.	Buy in hay for winter		Worm	
Sept.	Re-shoe / Re-seed pasture if necessary and if not done in the spring			Buy in straw for winter / Spread farmyard manure
Oct.	Worm	Re-shoe; decrease work-load and hard feed; decrease grooming		Continue roughing off
Nov.	Rasp teeth; Flu/tetanus vaccinations	Remove shoes and trim feet; horse turned away to rest	Service/maintenance of horse-box or vehicle and trailer	Worm, including bots
Dec.	New Zealand rugs for turned out horses	Hedging, fencing and ditching; stable maintenance and equipment repairs		Feet trimmed

Fig 48   Annual management programme for a pleasure or competition horse in work mainly during summer.

particularly virulent disease and modern vaccinations give protection against all known strains. Occasionally new strains occur and new vaccines have to be developed to combat them. Vaccinations against influenza were introduced to combat epidemics which disrupted racing, and the other competitive disciplines soon followed suit. Now it is virtually impossible to take an unvaccinated horse to shows and events. Reports of horses reacting adversely to such vaccinations have not been substantiated and provided you follow the recommended precaution of resting your horse for at least a week following his vaccination, there should be no problems. The initial course of vaccinations must be followed up with booster shots within each successive twelve month period, subject to any changes in Jockey Club or FEI (Fédération Equestre Internationale) regulations.

	WEEK 1	WEEK 2	WEEK 3	WEEK 4
Jan.		Third clip		
Feb.	Re-shoe	Fourth clip if required and coat has not started to slip		
Mar.		Re-shoe		
Apr.	Reduce work and hard feed; increase bulk; reduce grooming	Reduce blankets	Teeth rasped if necessary; flu and tetanus vaccinations	Remove shoes, trim feet and turn horse away to rest; use New Zealand rug until weather warm and summer coat through
May				
June	Trim feet			
July	Trim feet			
Aug.	Horse brought in to start fitness training; teeth rasped; feet trimmed and shod	Horse may be in at night, out during day; vice versa if weather is hot		
Sept.		Re-shoe; end of basic fitness training	Cub hunting starts; continue exercise on non-hunting days; one rest day a week	Horse usually stabled but turned out for several hours on non-hunting days
Oct.	Horse rugged at night as grooming is stepped up		Re-shoe	Full clip or hunter clip; rug day and night; additional blanket when clipped
Nov.	Opening meet			Re-shoe
Dec.	Second clip, usually a hunter clip			Re-shoe

Fig 49 Annual management programme for a hunter; note the difference from the management of a horse working in summer.

7 . Diet

INTRODUCTION

The food and water your horse consumes serve several purposes. Primarily, they sustain life. Without water the horse would become dehydrated, his vital systems would cease to function and he would eventually die. Food provides the energy that keeps the horse warm and enables him to move around. It also provides the materials that are needed for growth and development and for the repair and maintenance of the body's tissues.

How well these needs are met in the wild depends upon the availability of good food, primarily grass, at varying times of the year. Frequently nature does not provide enough good food, hence the poor condition of many moorland ponies in late winter and spring in Britain, or the difficulties for horses living in drought conditions in other countries.

Food required for these purposes is known as food at a 'maintenance' level. In other words, it is enough to keep a horse in a healthy condition when he is not answering the additional demands of being used by man, for riding or other work.

This brings us to the final purpose for which a horse needs food: to provide the energy needed for work. The amount of energy required, and thus the amount of extra feed, varies considerably according to the amount and level of work that the horse is doing. The type of feed also varies — sometimes extra protein may be required, for example in breeding stock, or sometimes extra carbohydrates or fats, when speed and stamina are important in competition.

The horse has a comparatively small stomach, with a considerable length of intestines, where much of the digestive process takes place. The whole of the digestive system comprises the mouth, throat, gullet, stomach, small intestine and large intestine. The digestive process is continuous and to keep it functioning efficiently, the horse must eat frequently and consume large amounts of fibre, or roughage, most of which is not digested, but helps other food to pass through the digestive system.

The food that provides the major part of this fibre is described as 'bulk' food. The working horse, however, also needs foods that provide extra energy and these are termed 'concentrates', 'short feed' or 'hard feed'.

In nutritional terms, bulk and concentrates are not mutually exclusive. Feed that contains most of the indigestible fibre, which is in fact carbohydrate, also contains other nutrients, such as digestible carbohydrate (sugars and starches), proteins, vitamins and minerals. These bulk foods include grass, hay, silage, ensiled hay, barn-dried grass, lucerne or alfalfa, oat straw and other palatable greens, bran and sugar beet pulp.

Likewise, concentrates include a certain amount of fibre (both digestible and indigestible), in addition to their main nutritive constituents of protein, digestible carbohydrate, fats, vitamins and minerals.

The horse in the wild obtains most of his nutrients from bulk feed, although he may find more concentrated sustenance in wild corn, seed heads of certain grasses, or from other sources. The division into concentrates and bulk is simply a convenient way for man to assess his horse's nutritional needs. Concentrate feeds include oats, barley, maize, peas and beans, corn oil, linseed, molasses, milk and eggs. They also include proprietary compound feeds, such as coarse mixes and cubes, which are usually classified according to the type of horse to which they will be fed (for example, racehorse cubes, event cubes, stud cubes, horse and pony cubes). These proprietary feeds are usually marketed as a complete, balanced ration, including the addition of a broad spectrum vitamin and mineral supplement. They should therefore not be fed mixed with other traditional concentrate feeds as this could cause an unbalanced diet, with consequent health, performance or digestive problems.

BASIC DIET

The metabolisms of horses are as individual as those of human beings. It is not possible to lay down an exact formula for feeding a specific type and size of horse, doing a specific amount of work. Apart from the individual needs of the horse, there are other variables, such as the state of the available grazing at different times of the year and changes in the horse's work-load at different times. His food must be adjusted if he is sick, or if he is being rested for any reason and, in adjusting his diet, his work-load, fitness level, health, and the method of his management must all be taken into account. Any changes in the horse's diet

must be made gradually, to allow for adjustments to the bacterial activity in the gut which aids the digestive process.

Quantities

Feeding is an art, rather than an exact science, and if your horse spends a fair amount of time at grass, you will have no way of accurately measuring the weight of food he consumes each day. However, the basic guide is that a horse will eat approximately 2.5 per cent of his body weight, for maintenance purposes, each day. The average 15.2hh. riding horse will weigh approximately 1,000lb (453.6kg). Therefore, the basic amount of food required can be calculated as 25lb (11.3kg).

Another accepted rule of thumb is that twice the horse's height is equal to the amount of food required in pounds. Therefore a 15.2hh. horse requires approximately 31lb food.

These two methods give a variation of 6lb in

Fig 50 A healthy horse in good summer condition. Note the sheen on her coat.

Fig 51   Native ponies can easily become overweight on summer grazing.

the total weight of food required by a 15.2hh. horse. This does not matter greatly when you appreciate that such calculations merely give you a starting point for working out a diet, and when you consider the enormous variations in breed and type that can occur in a 15.2hh. riding horse. You could be dealing with a choosy Thoroughbred, a part-bred hunter who needs feeding up to keep fit, a chunky cob who lives happily on pony nuts, or even one of those hardy types who expand visibly whenever they look at a blade of grass. So don't search for fixed rules in the hope of making the job easier — look at your horse instead and learn to recognise when he looks right and when he looks too fat or too thin, or out of condition in some other way. (*See* Chapter 15 for further discussion of this subject.)

Bulk and Concentrates

Having arrived at an approximate idea of the total quantity of food your horse will need, the next step is to divide it into bulk and concentrates. If the horse in the wild eats mainly bulk food, it follows logically that the more work a horse is expected to do and the fitter he is required to become, the more concentrates he will need in relation to bulk, to provide the energy to enable him to do his job.

Like the wild horse, the resting horse needs plenty of bulk, but provided the bulk is of good quality, he needs little, if anything, in the way of concentrates. From late spring to early autumn the horse kept at grass doing little work should not require extra food, but in winter, when the nutritional value of the grass is poor, he will need hay and a small amount of hard feed to maintain good condition.

The horse used mainly for pleasure riding and hacking should not need extra feed in summer if he has access to good grazing, but in winter will need hay and rather more hard food than the resting horse if he is to continue to work.

Hunters and competition horses are fed

according to their level of fitness, the hard feed being increased and the bulk reduced as they become fitter and as the work-load is increased, and vice versa when the work-load is reduced as they are 'let down'. A fit hunter or eventer at the height of the season might be getting as much as 16 to 20lb (7.3 to 9.1kg) of concentrates a day, divided into four or five feeds. Such a horse is unlikely to be turned out for more than an hour or two a day and will be getting between 10 and 14lb (4.5 and 6.5kg) of hay to make up his total ration.

Overfeeding

At this point a word of warning is necessary. Overfeeding of horses causes just as many problems as underfeeding. Some problem areas include:

1. The combination of overweight animals and fresh spring grass, often resulting in laminitis.
2. Overfeeding of young stock with the resultant excess weight causing pressure on growing limbs and joints.
3. The combination of too much food and too little exercise in hunters, competition and riding horses, which can cause temperament and handling problems as well as azoturia, if the horse is suddenly brought back into work after being laid off without a corresponding reduction in food.
4. Overfeeding of pregnant mares, which can lead to difficult foaling.
5. Indiscriminate use of vitamin supplements, some of which can be toxic in excessive amounts.

The golden rule for riding and competition horses is always to increase the exercise level ahead of the feed level and, when letting down, decrease the feed before you decrease the exercise.

Take the time just to stand and watch your horse, in the stable and in the field. Learn to notice slight changes in his condition − the size of his gut, how well covered he is, how his muscles develop as he becomes fitter. In winter, if your horse is not clipped, it is easy to mistake a thick coat for good condition, as even if he has lost condition, his coat may hide his ribs. If his condition is satisfactory, his loins will be flat and well covered. Place your hand across his back, just behind the saddle position. If the loins are solid and flat, all well and good, if they fall away from your hand, the horse needs more food.

PLANNING A DIET

How much food should the riding horse be given, assuming he is used mainly for pleasure hacking, ridden three to five times a week, with the occasional weekend riding club competition?

Working on the basis that he is a 15.2hh. part-bred, from the formulae outlined earlier, we would expect to feed him a total of around 25-30lb (11.3-13.6kg) food each day. Assuming also that he is living out, he will obtain a considerable proportion of this from grass in summer, although in winter the contribution of the grass is greatly reduced. Initially, if you know what was fed before you acquired the horse, continue with that, and after a week or two you should be able to assess how well the diet suits him. Alternatively, you may want to make changes, to take account of his new work-load, for example. If you do not know what has been fed you can work out a diet as follows:

Summer

Good grazing provides the major part of the diet; hay is only necessary if the horse is being kept in for any reason. Assess the horse's condition on arrival and initially feed concentrates only if he is in poor condition. Start with a small amount, perhaps 4lb (1.8kg) per day, in two feeds, and use either traditional feed (1lb (0.5kg) rolled oats, 1lb (0.5kg) cooked flaked barley, mixed with a handful of chaff, or bran if chaff is not available, for each feed), or use a proprietary feed such as horse and pony mix or cubes, in amounts recommended by the manufacturer. Do not give vitamin and mineral supplements, as the grass should provide all that is necessary, but a salt lick can be placed in the field.

If the horse is in good condition, do not feed concentrates until you see how he copes on grass alone. After a week or two you will be able to tell if he is maintaining his condition, or needs additional food to cope with his work-load, in which case introduce concentrates as described above, gradually increasing the quantity until the required condition and performance is achieved. However, a horse being ridden three to five times a week, with the occasional competition should not need extra food once the spring grass arrives and any horse on good pasture who fails to put on condition should be examined for other health problems. The most likely cause is parasitic worms. Even when wormed fairly regularly, horses kept on ground where there is a heavy worm burden can occasionally suffer from a severe infestation, which requires treatment by a veterinary surgeon.

Winter

The horse will be kept in at night, out during the day. Hay is best fed ad lib, in hay-nets, that is, as much hay as the horse can eat − it replaces the quantities of grass he consumed in summer. In general, hay contains less nourishment than summer grass, so more concentrates will be needed. Introduce them gradually if the horse has not been accustomed to concentrate feed, even if the horse is in poor condition to start with. To build up condition, use fattening foods such as cooked flaked barley, and soaked sugar beet pulp (a bulk food, but it will help put weight on and has a slightly laxative effect so is useful for a stabled horse who is receiving mainly dry food). The addition of milk powder will also help, plus a broad spectrum vitamin and mineral supplement containing lysine, which is an important body-building amino acid. Alternatively, you could use stud cubes, which have a higher protein level than other compound feeds and should help improve poor condition, but remember not to mix them with other concentrates.

If the horse is in good condition, with the work level described above, 6 to 10lb (2.7 to 4.5kg) of concentrates per day, in two feeds, should see him safely through the winter, adjusted as necessary. The properties of the various feedstuffs commonly used for horses are listed in Appendix I.

FEEDING THE COMPETITION HORSE

The higher the performance expected from a horse, the more critical is his feeding routine, and the more closely related it becomes to his work-load, training programme and state of fitness. This applies whatever the discipline involved, be it showjumping, eventing, racing, endurance riding, dressage or driving. It applies to a slightly less critical extent to hunters and, for rather different reasons, to show horses.

Hunters

The hunter is required to be moderately fit throughout the hunting season. His programme involves sufficient exercise to get him fit enough to stay out hunting all day, two or three times a week, with enough speed and stamina to keep up with the field during a run, but without necessarily reaching the absolute peak of athletic performance. His feeding is based on traditional lines, which, in general, have proved their suitability for the purpose. The hunter is usually kept stabled once he is 'brought up' from his summer's rest and by the time of the opening meet his diet will probably consist of a minimum of 60 per cent concentrates to 40 per cent bulk. After hunting and on rest days, he will be given a bran mash (a warm mash made with bran, with salt added, boiling water poured over it and left to cool slightly) which may be made more palatable by the addition of some sliced carrots or molasses. This acts as a purgative and although it is still widely used, its value is questionable, especially since the high phosphorus : calcium ratio of bran has been linked with various health problems, in particular muscle disorders.

Show Horses

The show horse needs to be fit enough to cope with the rigours and tension of travelling and parading in the show ring, sometimes several times in one day. To be successful he also needs to be in 'show condition'. In terms of weight, this is often unfortunately interpreted as fat, rather than well fleshed, and the result is often joint and leg problems caused by carrying excessive bodyweight, particularly in young stock being shown in hand. A good show judge will not be impressed by a fat horse, nor will the excess coverage blind him to conformation faults – to produce a horse in the correct condition for showing takes considerable skill. Apart from weight, the show horse's coat and skin must be in excellent condition, shining and healthy. Various foods help to promote healthy skin and hair, including linseed jelly, eggs and supplements containing the amino acid methionine (which also acts in conjunction with biotin and zinc to promote healthy horn growth). Eggs can be added to the diet before a show, but should not be fed on a regular basis as they contain a substance which destroys vitamins.

Performance Horses

Feeding the performance horse so that he can compete to the best of his ability is an essential part of the trainer's skill. The basic principles are the same as for any horse, but the skill begins in when and how the diet should be adjusted, in conjunction with the training programme, to arrive at peak fitness for a particular competition.

Sporting or athletic performance involves the athlete's body being subjected to a considerable degree of stress. This means that any weaknesses in the body's systems will sooner or later be discovered as they affect the horse's performance and health. The healthy adult horse requires

Fig 52   A fit event horse. He will be stabled most of the time and given a high-concentrate diet.

approximately 8 per cent protein in his diet. However, proprietary feeds for competition horses usually contain between 10 and 14 per cent protein, the theory being that extra protein is needed for tissue development and for the repair of the extra wear and tear on the horse's body. Whilst young, developing horses and those who are recovering from debilitating injury or illness may benefit from extra protein, the general principle of feeding high protein diets to working horses is of doubtful value, as any proteins not used for growth or tissue repair are converted for energy production or stored as fat until needed. Energy can be produced more cheaply and efficiently from other nutrients.

Proteins are made up of various amino acids, some of which are manufactured within the horse's body, whilst others, the 'essential amino acids', must be obtained from food. These include lysine and methionine.

The main energy-producing nutrients are carbohydrates, in the form of sugars, starches and fibre. Immediately available energy is produced by the conversion of sugars and starches into glucose, those not needed immediately being stored as fat. Most of the fibre, which comes from the stalky parts of grass and hay, assists other food to pass through the system.

Fats provide concentrated energy in a higher density form than carbohydrate and research has shown that endurance horses benefit from increased levels of unsaturated fats in their feed. Fats may be given in the form of vegetable oil added to the feed and can be useful when a horse refuses to eat sufficient cereals to achieve the energy output required. A high fat diet will only benefit a fit, hard-working horse, as the animal's ability to utilise fats increases with training.

Vitamin and mineral supplements are rarely needed for the non-competing horse, as the basic diet will provide enough of the minute amounts required for growth, repair of body tissues and the healthy functioning of the body's systems. However, many horse owners like to give their horses a broad spectrum supplement, that is, one containing balanced amounts of all the necessary vitamins, minerals and trace elements,

particularly in winter. Provided the recommended dosage is adhered to, this will do no harm and the horse may have a generally improved mien.

For competition horses, however, deficiencies may occur where the horse is being fed a largely cereal diet in an artificial environment. For example, cereals are deficient in calcium but high in phosphorus. Too high a phosphorus content in the diet will affect the body's ability to absorb calcium, which is essential for the healthy development and strength of bone, so a calcium supplement may be advisable. Vitamin D is also required for the absorption of calcium and is mainly produced by the action of sunlight on a horse's skin, so if a horse is seldom turned out, extra Vitamin D may be indicated.

Most vitamins and trace elements are toxic if overfed, so if a deficiency is suspected it is important to consult your veterinary surgeon and obtain a proper diagnosis of what is wrong, before adding supplements to the feed. Also, vitamins and minerals interact with each other in complex ways, and if an owner feeds an assortment of unrelated supplements based on guesswork, serious problems can result. (For essential vitamins and minerals and more information on the properties and uses of foodstuffs, see Appendix I.)

FEED PREPARATION AND QUALITY CONTROL

Some horses are fastidious feeders; others will consume everything offered, plus anything else they can find, from their straw bedding to the top of the stable door. For the sake of the horse's health it is essential to provide food of as good quality as you can obtain and this is particularly important with regard to hay. The mould spores present in hay and straw frequently cause respiratory problems in stabled horses. Not all horses are susceptible enough to these moulds to start coughing, but even so, performance is affected to a certain extent.

All hay fed to horses should be of good quality,

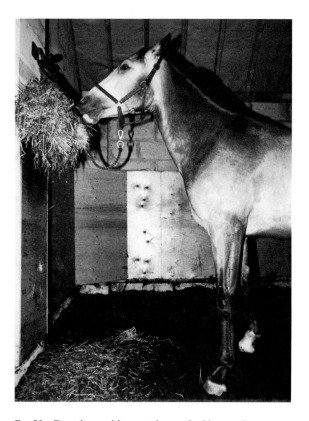

Fig 53 Dust-free stabling, with peat bedding and the horse fed on soaked hay or haylage.

Grain bought from a reputable feed merchant should be clean, free from pollutants and of the best quality available. If it is not all you would wish (for example, small grains of oats, containing too much husk), you will have to feed extra to make up the food value – the amounts will have to be deduced by observation.

Prepare your feeds to suit your horse. It is always a good idea to feed concentrates (except proprietary cubes and mixes) dampened down. This mixes the feed better, especially if powdered additives are being used, and helps prevent the horse from being too selective. It will also help prevent choking caused by dry food getting stuck in the gullet, but the concentrates should not be wet and sloppy as this might encourage the horse to gobble his feed too quickly.

It is good practice to use a bulk food as a 'mixer', to prevent the meal being eaten too quickly, which could cause indigestion. The ideal mixer is chaff, that is, a combination of chopped hay and oat straw, or even hay alone, but this may not be possible if you do not possess or have access to a chaff cutter. Molassed chaff is available in proprietary form, but is comparatively expensive.

Another good 'mixer' is soaked sugar beet pulp, especially for stabled horses in winter, as it helps to keep weight on, is high in calcium and has a slightly laxative effect. In these respects it does a similar job to grass, so is superfluous as a mixer if you are feeding a horse at grass in summer.

The traditionally used mixer is broad bran. However, good quality broad bran is virtually impossible to obtain nowadays, owing to modern milling processes. The link between bran and a calcium:phosphorus imbalance has discouraged its continued use, as already mentioned. If you do use bran, keep the quantities small, and if you are feeding it to a primarily stabled horse on a cereal diet, consider giving a balanced calcium supplement to prevent any problems.

whether it is meadow hay or seed hay, but if your horse shows any signs of a dust allergy, all his hay should be well soaked, by thorough immersion in clean water. Alternatively, one of the ensiled hays, or 'haylage', can be fed instead. These are made in slightly varying ways, but the principle is to bale the hay when the grass has wilted but before it has completely dried out, using a special process to prevent heating and to compress and seal the bales so that all the goodness is retained. Ensiled hay has a higher nutritional value than ordinary hay, so fewer concentrates are required.

Good quality grain, especially oats, can sometimes be difficult to obtain, which is why some owners prefer to use compound feeds. However, in compound feeds the ingredients may vary from batch to batch, which may cause upsets, even though the actual nutritional analysis is unchanged.

FEEDING PROBLEMS

Overweight

This most often occurs in children's ponies of the hardy native type, who are able to live on relatively sparse grazing, but are kept in lush paddocks and not given sufficient exercise. They put on weight extremely quickly when the spring grass arrives and there is a serious risk of laminitis ('founder' in the United States), unless care is taken to restrict their grazing. The important thing is to prevent the problem before it occurs: take the pony off the grass before he starts to expand round the middle. Sometimes drastic measures are required when a pony becomes seriously overweight and although ideally he eats almost continually, it may be necessary to restrict his grazing to an hour in the morning and an hour in the evening. Preferably, however, he should be moved to a relatively bare paddock where he will not have access to so much rich grass.

Gobbling

Eating too quickly is not good for your horse's digestive system, nor for your pocket, as apart from giving your horse indigestion, quantities of food will pass through his system undigested and will thus be wasted. Using mixers is one way of preventing this. It also helps to give smaller feeds, more frequently, so that the horse does not have the opportunity to eat a large amount of concentrates in one go.

Fussy Feeders

This is a problem that can only be resolved by trial and error. Find out by a process of elimination if there is a particular ingredient that the horse objects to. Can it be replaced by something more to his taste? Can it be disguised in some way to make it more palatable? For example, molasses mixed with water and poured over the feed may help; some horses develop a taste for cider vinegar, which can then be used to disguise almost anything. Sliced carrots or apples may make the feed more tempting – they must always be sliced lengthways, not in chunks, as otherwise they may get stuck in the gullet and cause choking.

Refusal to Eat

This is a rather different problem and usually one that has an underlying cause. It frequently occurs in horses who have been stabled and in hard work for some considerable time. They may respond to a change in diet, or there may be a health problem, or they may simply need a rest and a change. If in doubt, consult your veterinary surgeon and turn the horse out as much as possible.

Quidding

This is the term used to describe a horse who spits his food out from the side of his mouth, usually dry food or balled up hay mixed with saliva. The most common reason is trouble with the teeth which is preventing the horse from chewing up his food properly. Alternatively, an obstruction in the throat may be the cause. Call your veterinary surgeon, who will attend to the horse's teeth as necessary, or otherwise diagnose the cause.

Choking

This usually occurs when the horse has swallowed some dry food, such as bread or insufficiently soaked sugar beet, which has swollen up and blocked the entrance to the stomach at the end of the oesophagus. The situation may look alarming and the horse may appear very uncomfortable, trying to dislodge the blockage, possibly with mucus and bits of food running back from his nose. Often the horse will manage to dislodge the blockage himself, but, for safety's sake, call the vet and usually the outcome will be a happy one.

The situation may be much more serious if the horse has swallowed some foreign object (which is possible but unlikely), or, as sometimes happens, the horse has got into the feed bin, or has mistakenly been fed some dry sugar beet. Be very careful to avoid this, it is frequently fatal. It is worth repeating that sugar beet, whether shreds or nuts, must be soaked for a minimum of 24 hours in sufficient cold water to rehydrate it completely, before being fed to horses.

Experience will tell you how much water to use to make the sugar beet soaked but not sloppy. As a rough guide, use approximately twice the volume of water to dried sugar beet. If boiling water is used, the soaking time can be reduced, but should never be less than 12 hours.

8 . Handling

UNDERSTANDING YOUR HORSE

The thing that marks out a good horseman is not how many rosettes there are on his wall, nor how big and grand his stables are, nor how much his horses cost him, but how well he understands the horse. A good horseman may well be a successful showman or competitor, because his understanding will give him the advantage of knowing how to get the best from his horses. A good horseman will get more from a mediocre horse than a poor one will get from the best bred, most beautiful looking animal that money can buy. Understanding the horse is the key to successful management in every way.

In the horse world can be found people at both extremes of the spectrum. On the one hand there are those whose sole interest lies in winning prizes. If they don't succeed with a particular horse, they sell him and buy another, until he too, through mismanagement and mishandling, stops winning. Such owners waste a lot of money and miss the vast amount of pleasure that can be had from the satisfaction of a job well done.

At the other extreme are those who make the mistake of endowing the horse with human attributes which he simply does not have. The horse is treated as one of the family, and whilst there is nothing wrong in that, the mistake lies in expecting the horse to behave and react with human reason and logic. This type of owner is obviously preferable to the type who treats his horse as a prize-winning machine, but he becomes confused when his horse fails to behave in what he sees as a reasonable and logical manner. The ensuing problems are entirely the result of a lack of communication between two completely unrelated species — horse and man.

Managing the Horse's Instincts

The horse has many attributes which distinguish him from man and from other species; in particular he is superior to man in two ways — he has greater strength and greater speed. In the distant past, man learned to dominate the horse and harness this power and speed for his own ends. The wild horse is a social creature, living a herd existence, with a strongly defined 'pecking order'. Very early in his life, he learns his own place in the order, and even in a small group of domesticated horses sharing a field, a definite leader will emerge, the others falling into line according to seniority, strength or aggressiveness. The horse's natural acceptance of a social order made the task of domestication easier as, once dominated, the horse is inclined to accept his lot quite willingly for most of the time.

Although you might think of your horse as a friend, therefore, the relationship is necessarily one of domination, and to be successful, the owner or handler must be the dominant party, or leader, not the horse! If this sounds too obvious to mention, think of all the frustrated humans you have seen attempting to control decidedly dominant horses.

Dominating your horse, however, does not mean beating him into submission, but simply exerting your will over the horse's possibly different will. Those who use force frequently find it rebounding on themselves, as the horse quickly associates the human being with pain and resents all efforts to control him. Since the horse is much stronger than the human, a so-called 'dangerous' horse is often the result.

The horse in the herd follows the herd's leaders; if he does not, he is quickly driven into place as the safety of the herd depends upon it. As the young males grow up, the stallion drives them from the herd, before they mature enough to

Fig 54   Harnessing strength.

become a serious threat to his leadership. Bands of these colts often stay together for safety, and even they will establish a pecking order of their own. The horse looks for a social structure in which to live and if a human being, whom he learns to trust, is part of that structure, he will accept that person's leadership.

This should be the basis of all your dealings with your horse – to teach him to trust you and have confidence in you, whilst showing him quite firmly that you are in charge.

To do this requires forethought and anticipation. Everything a horse does is based on patterns of behaviour evolved over the centuries to ensure the survival of his species. The most important of these patterns, from the point of view of handling the horse, is his urge to flee from danger, flight being his best defence. When you appreciate that to a horse everything unknown represents danger, it is easy to see the importance of teaching the horse to trust his handler.

Associated with the freedom to flee, is the horse's need for open space where he can see far and wide, coupled with his fear of restricted spaces, where he cannot see what hidden dangers there may be, and his fear of being tied up so that his ability to move is curtailed.

Horse Physiology

You should also try to understand the effect of how the horse's physiology differs from that of the human being. For example, by raising or lowering his head, he can see for long distances, but he cannot see something directly in front of his nose. His vision is quite complicated; when he tilts his head, he is not being difficult, just trying to get a better look at something. This is why a horse travelling over rough ground should be allowed to get his head down, where he can see the going underfoot. He also has a blind area directly behind him, which is why a horse startled by someone or something approaching from the rear might leap away or kick out.

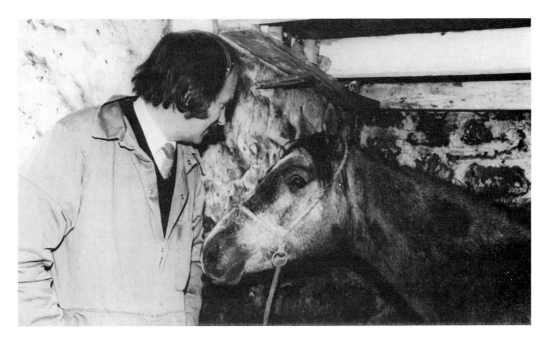

Fig 55 This young horse is nervous of being handled. Here he stretches out his nose to touch and perhaps smell the stranger, his ears pricked forward, listening and his eyes wide open, wary and alert.

Fig 56 Here the nervous horse focuses his attention back to the hand on his neck and whatever may be going to happen to him. Note the ears turned back to catch sounds from behind.

The horse has sharper hearing than the human and can swivel his ears to pick up a sound from a particular direction. His ears are also used to display his feelings — pricked to show interest in what lies ahead, drooping when relaxed, turned back to listen to his rider, or to sounds from behind, and flat back in annoyance or anger. He also uses his senses of taste and smell to give him information about food, other objects with which he comes into contact, and his general surroundings.

Ear movements, along with movements of his head, nose and mouth, and his body movements and attitude, are the horse's means of communicating with his handler and the more you observe them and the better you learn to understand them, the easier it will be to handle your horse successfully and without problems.

How can you use all this information to help you handle your horse well? Basically, you must look at each situation from the horse's point of view, anticipate how a horse would be likely to react and as far as possible introduce any new experience in such a way as to avoid frightening him or making him resistant to what you want him to do. The first essential is to gain his trust.

GOOD HANDLING PRINCIPLES

In any relationship, trust cannot be won overnight, but develops over a period of time. A horse who has always been well and kindly handled will work on the principle that any new human with whom he comes into contact can be trusted until he proves otherwise. A horse who has been badly treated will take the opposite attitude. It is obviously of the utmost importance that a young horse, undergoing his early training, should be properly handled, as lessons learned at this stage will be strongly imprinted and will help to shape his attitude for the rest of his life.

The key to effective communication with your horse is patience. This applies at all stages of development and training, whether you are teaching a youngster that letting you touch him won't do him any harm, or whether you are teaching a difficult movement to an advanced dressage horse. The horse needs time to absorb the lesson he is being taught — to think about it, understand it and remember it for the future.

Messages from the handler to the horse must be given clearly. It is no good telling him more or less what you want, as he does not have the power of reason necessary to interpret an inaccurate signal as a precise command. If you want him to respond precisely, you must give him unmistakably clear instructions and, don't forget, they must be instructions that a horse's mind can understand. For riding the horse, the aids were developed by the classical horsemasters to make as much use as possible of the horse's natural physical reactions to the stimuli of the rider's weight, seat, body, leg and hand movements. The whip and spur are artificial extensions of these aids. Similar stimuli are used from the ground to teach the horse how to behave in the stable, or whenever he is being handled in hand rather than under saddle.

To communicate with your horse, you need to

Fig 57 Building a relationship, the aids must be clear and precise.

have his attention, which is impossible if he is disturbed or frightened in any way. Horses quickly pick up the mood and attitude of the people around them, especially anyone riding or handling them. If a horse's handler is nervous, excited, or alarmed, the horse instantly interprets this as the handler's response to something frightening, even if he himself cannot see the cause of the fear. His own immediate response is to become alarmed or nervous too, and his attention is distracted completely from the job in hand. Only in extremely rare cases will a horse become vicious towards his handler on his own account; in general it will not occur to him that he could be the cause of his handler's fear or nervousness.

If the handler becomes angry or loses his temper, the horse will usually react in one of two ways — he will either be cowed and frightened by the anger, or he will resent it and become angry himself. In the latter case, depending upon the situation, he may become sullen, stubborn and resentful, or he may resist by fighting his handler and throwing himself around. Neither situation produces the desired result.

Anger, fear and nervousness on the part of the handler are therefore all bars to communication and can easily result in the horse learning the opposite lesson from what was intended. At all costs the handler must stay calm and unruffled, and must not show any nervousness to the horse.

The final requirement for successfully handling your horse is firmness. The horse is extremely sensitive to the human voice and to its various tones. The actual words used do not matter much, so long as they are consistent when giving instructions, but the tone of your voice is very important. The most useful tones include a low, soothing tone (including humming, singing or whistling softly) to settle a nervous horse; casual, firm, matter of fact tones for giving everyday commands such as 'move over', 'pick up' and 'walk on'; and a loud, strong tone to discourage bad behaviour — but not the high-pitched shriek that is so often heard wherever horses are gathered together. It startles the horse and everyone else in earshot, but the horse is unlikely

to associate it with his behaviour, whereas a loud, strong 'No!', delivered at close quarters, will often do the trick. Tones that show exasperation, nervousness or any lack of self-control will have the same effect on the horse as other displays of fear, nervousness or anger.

Firmness should be manifest in all handling of your horse. This does not mean that you behave like a drill sergeant, simply that your movements around the horse should be purposeful, positive and confident. For example, if you are grooming him, use firm but gentle strokes: don't tickle him with the brush; don't fumble when you adjust your tack; and don't make sudden unexpected movements when you are close to him, such as waving your hand in front of his face to greet someone across the yard. Always remain aware of your horse and what he is doing at any moment, and avoid startling him. Treat him as though you expect good behaviour and he will frequently oblige. If he misbehaves, show him gently but firmly that bad manners will not be tolerated.

To sum up, these are the qualities required for a competent handler:

1. Common sense and forethought — plan what you are going to do in detail, then do it.
2. Anticipation — consider the situation from the horse's point of view and arrange matters accordingly.
3. Patience — give yourself time to communicate with the horse so that he understands what you want, and give him time to absorb the lesson.
4. Clarity — be precise and consistent with your commands.
5. Calmness — avoid the emotional barriers to communication which are set up by fear, nervousness and anger.
6. Firmness — use your voice and actions to insist quietly on good behaviour.

Firmness is probably the most difficult aspect of handling for the new horse owner, as it must be used in proportion to the horse's reaction to whatever is being asked of him. The degree of firmness necessary in any situation is something that the handler can only learn through experience.

GOOD HANDLING PRACTICE

Having discussed the principles behind successful handling of your horse, building up trust and confidence and developing a good working relationship, how do we put those principles into practice?

Most foals born destined to become riding horses become used to human contact from a very early age and never have to overcome the fear of human beings, who represent an unknown danger. Horses born to a life in the herd will take much longer to accept the close proximity of man. The first horse you buy, ready broken and schooled, should not have any objection to being approached by a new human being, but when you first walk up to him, remember that you want him to think of you as an honorary horse, albeit a dominant one.

Walk up to him slowly, but steadily and obliquely, approaching his shoulder, not his head, so that he can get a good look at you. Speak to him quietly. Stroke his shoulder or scratch his withers (something horses do quite vigorously for each other) and let him sniff at and nuzzle you. This is his way of getting more information about you than he can see with his eyes. A well-trained horse will accept your presence quickly and with equanimity, and probably won't be very interested in you once he has assured himself you are not dangerous. Now is not the time to produce a titbit from your pocket. A horse who is taught to expect too many titbits becomes a persistent nuisance and the habit should be discouraged. The place for titbits is as an occasional reward for good behaviour, although a caress will do as well, or as a rare treat when you visit him in his field. They are also useful in rewarding a horse who is being taught something new, such as loading, or to stand quietly for the vet.

Horses communicate in very physical ways — nuzzling, sniffing, blowing, lip wrinkling, licking, nipping and rubbing against you may all be expressions of affection, companionship or

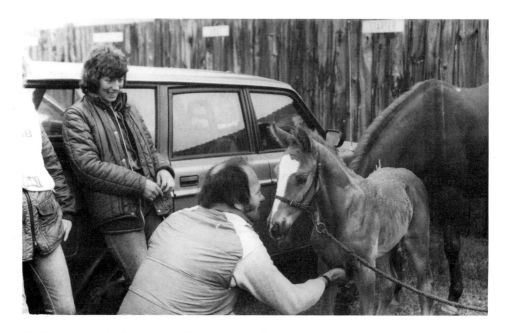

Fig 58   Making friends. Most foals become used to human contact at an early age.

simply the horse's natural social behaviour. Less friendly expressions may include tail swishing (in annoyance rather than to flick away flies), biting, stamping, kicking and charging.

Horses also communicate vocally. Nothing is more rewarding than the low nicker of welcome you receive when your horse has learned to like and trust you. Then there is the slightly more demanding whinny when you appear with the feed bucket, the shrill neigh of horses calling to each other across a boundary hedge and the warning nicker a mare may give to a too adventurous foal. A horse may squeal in temper or annoyance or grunt in pain and a stallion will scream his rage and defiance when challenged by another.

Most of these means of expression will become familiar to you as your horse uses them, and you will work out your own responses.

Catching

One of the things that often worries new horse owners is how to catch a horse who has been turned out into a field. Some horses obligingly trot up to the gate and thrust their heads into a waiting headcollar. Others are less co-operative and a little psychology is needed. Ideally, you don't want to have to take feed with you to tempt a horse to come to you in the field, but this can be a useful ploy at times. When the horse has forgotten his objections to being caught, the bucket can be replaced with a titbit in the hand and eventually dispensed with altogether. Such problems may recur if the horse's routine is altered, for example if he is left in the field for a longer period of time than usual.

To catch your horse, walk up to him as normal, approaching him at his shoulder. Do not walk so quickly that he is startled, nor so slowly that he loses interest and turns away before you reach him. If he does turn away, simply repeat the procedure. If his intention not to be caught becomes more obvious, for example if he trots away at speed, employ the titbit method. When you reach the horse's side, slowly slip your arm around his neck and pass the strap of the headcollar into your right hand, so that if he moves to get away you can hold him firmly around his neck. Slip the nose-piece over his nose and do up the strap. Stroke him and praise him quietly.

Leading

To lead your horse, hold the lead rope close to his head in your right hand, standing on his left side, and loosely coil the slack in your left hand. Never wrap the rope around your hand. Any sudden movement of the horse could at best cause you rope burns, and at worst pull you over and drag you along behind him. Ask the horse to walk forwards by moving on yourself, and at the same time saying firmly 'Walk on'. If the horse baulks at walking forwards, don't try to pull him along — remember he is stronger than you. Instead, push him sideways in a circle away from you. He will move his feet to prevent himself overbalancing, and this will usually get him walking. If he still refuses to walk, a tap on his quarters with a long schooling whip, held in your left hand so that you can reach behind without turning around, should

Fig 59   The right way to lead your horse.

produce movement. This should not be necessary with a schooled horse, although it is a recognised method of teaching young horses to lead.

Horses entering strange surroundings will want to assure themselves that there are no hidden dangers in them before committing themselves. A horse being taken into a new stable will therefore pause at the door, lower his head, peer inside and sniff the air before entering. This is a good example of a time to employ patience and give your horse a chance to reassure himself about anything new.

Tying Up

Once inside the stable you may wish to tie your horse up, to be groomed, for example. Teaching a horse to be tied up can be nerve-racking if incorrectly done, as he will initially be frightened at having his head movement restricted. It is essential to avoid a situation where the horse fights the tie rope, as in his panic he may throw himself about and injure himself, not to mention being put off being tied up for life.

At first it is a good idea simply to pass the rope through the tie ring and hold on to the end of it while you brush the horse quietly, thus giving him a chance to get used to the idea and at the same time being able to release him quickly if he becomes upset or pulls back. When this no longer bothers him, tie a piece of baler twine to the tie ring, then tie the horse up, using a quick release knot to attach the tie rope to the baler twine. The baler twine is used because it will break if the horse panics and pulls back, so avoiding a dangerous struggle and a broken headcollar.

Horses should never be tied directly to the metal tie ring. Do not tie the horse up so short that he cannot turn his head at all, nor so long that he can get his head under the rope or his feet over it. Always use a quick release knot (see Fig 60); for a horse accustomed to being tied up, the end of the rope can be slipped through the loop of the knot to prevent him untying himself and escaping! Avoid leaving your horse tied up unattended and never leave a young or nervous horse tied up without supervision.

Horses are usually handled from the left-hand (or near) side when being led, mounted or dismounted, the traditional reason being that it enabled a cavalry soldier to keep his sword hand free and the sword, on the left, out of the way when getting into the saddle. It is a good idea, as you are unlikely to be encumbered by a sword, to handle your horse from both sides, which may be useful at times and may also encourage even muscle development by preventing the horse from being always bent in the same direction.

STABLE MANNERS

A horse who is awkward in the stable is a nuisance, making it difficult for you to work round him so that you need twice as much time to get every job done. Therefore good stable manners are an essential part of training and, with a little perseverance, can be quite easily achieved with most horses.

First, be thoughtful in your stable routine. For example, don't try to muck out while your horse is eating his breakfast — you will only succeed in irritating him. When you are doing stable chores it is best to have your horse tied up so that you can move in and out of the box freely and you know exactly where the horse is at all times. Some aspects of stable manners are taught simply by repetition and patience, such as encouraging the horse to stand quietly whilst being groomed. If he does not like being brushed, use a softer brush and more gentle movements, until he learns to accept the process. Some thin-skinned horses will never accept vigorous brushing with a dandy brush. Remember that all horses are individuals and treating them all alike won't work.

Two commands that your horse needs to learn in the stable are to move over and to move back. To teach him to move over, stand beside him and press gently, just behind his girth, with your hand, just as you would with your leg if you were riding him. At the same time say firmly 'Over'. If he does not move, nudge him gently again and repeat the command until it has the desired effect. Eventually, he should move over to the

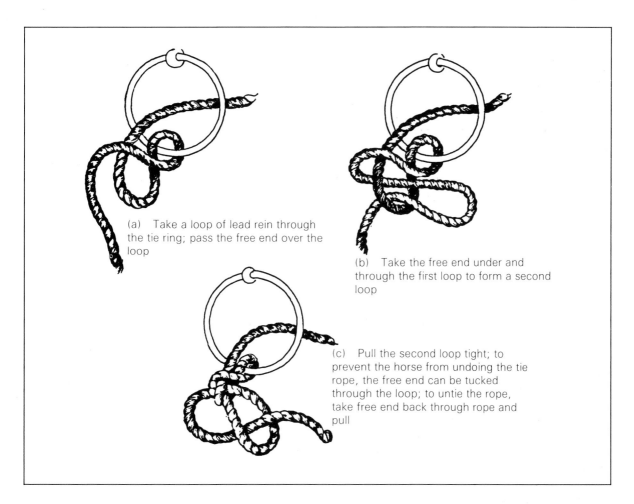

(a)   Take a loop of lead rein through the tie ring; pass the free end over the loop

(b)   Take the free end under and through the first loop to form a second loop

(c)   Pull the second loop tight; to prevent the horse from undoing the tie rope, the free end can be tucked through the loop; to untie the rope, take free end back through rope and pull

Fig 60 A quick-release knot.

spoken word only, or even to a click of your tongue as you stand beside him.

To move him back, stand in front of him and place one hand on each side of his headcollar. Press him back at the same time saying firmly 'Back'. If this does not work, try one hand on his nose and the other on his chest, just in front of the shoulder of whichever leg is farthest forward, repeating the command as press back. Again, he should eventually learn to respond to the spoken word only, or the word plus a light touch, which will be useful, for example, when you want to go into the stable with his feed.

Teaching the horse to pick up his feet on command is another necessary part of stable manners, both for you to pick them out each day and for the farrier who comes to shoe him. To pick up his near front foot, stand at his shoulder, facing his tail, bend and run your left hand down his leg, saying 'Pick it up' as you reach the pastern. Most horses will respond by picking up the foot to avoid the tickle of the hand running down the leg, and the lesson is quickly learned. Soon you will only need to bend towards the foot and the horse will pick it up to meet your hand, in response to the spoken command.

The same procedure is used for the hind leg and the safest place to stand is beside the horse, slightly in front of the hind leg, so that if he should by any chance kick out, you will be out of

Fig 61 When picking up the horse's feet, stand to one side and face the back of the horse.

harm's way. For the off-side feet you should use the right hand. The foot, once raised, should be held up for you by the horse in a relaxed manner, and you should speak quietly to him until he learns to do this.

The correct way to tack up will be discussed in Chapter 10, but your horse should also learn to stand quietly for the farrier, or veterinary surgeon. If he is inclined to fidget, the best way to hold him steady is to stand in front of him, with one hand firmly holding either side of his headcollar or bridle. However, do not place yourself directly in front of a horse who is likely to rear or lunge forward to avoid whatever is being done to him.

HANDLING PROBLEMS

How do you deal with the horse who is difficult to handle in certain situations? Ideally, if you have bought a well-trained horse, he will behave himself in any of the situations you are likely to encounter and handling problems might never occur. However, horses who are perfectly well behaved most of the time may object to various experiences, or develop bad habits, and if you know how to deal with them, the difficulty can be minimised.

A patient farrier is a great asset, but if your horse objects to being shod, you can get him more accustomed to the idea by spending some time in the stable, picking up his feet and tapping them gently, until the situation bores him rather than alarms him. When the farrier arrives make sure there is a dry, clear space for him to work in, so that he has room to manoeuvre without tools being sent flying. Provide a hay-net or some titbits to distract the horse from what is happening to him.

Routine visits by the vet can be a problem if your horse takes a dislike to having his teeth rasped, or to injections. A good veterinary surgeon will overcome the problem by firm but kindly handling, but it helps if the owner can be as firm. If the treatment your horse is getting upsets you, stay away and get someone else to help the vet. Otherwise you will only encourage the horse to become more nervous than necessary. If you are assisting the vet by holding the horse, don't get unnecessarily angry, shouting at your horse if he misbehaves. A firm 'No', followed by soothing tones and more positive handling are more helpful.

There is a difference between a horse who is genuinely frightened and one who is simply making a fuss. The former needs to be given time to consider the frightening object or situation and should be spoken to soothingly to show him that there is no need to worry. He will then usually accept what is happening and stand quietly. The latter may well need a sharp reprimand and a smack to overcome his resistance. Various considerations may govern the horse's reaction to what is happening to him. Is he young and the experience new? Is he just fidgeting about a regular routine? Is the treatment painful? Has a similar experience frightened him in the past?

As the horse is stronger than his handlers, some form of restraint might be advisable if he really continues to object violently to necessary treatment. The simplest and most commonly used method is the twitch. This is a short length of wood, with a hole drilled in one end, to which is attached a loop of string. The string is placed over the sensitive part of the nose and the handle turned until the string is twisted tight, thus holding the horse immobile. It used to be thought that this caused the horse greater pain than the treatment to which he was objecting and therefore made him stand still. However, recent research has indicated that twitching and similar stimuli result in the production of natural painkillers, known as endorphins, which cause the horse to relax temporarily and stand still. A

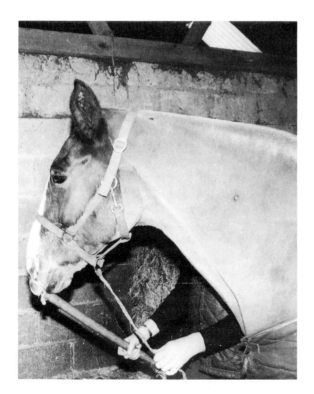

Fig 62 The twitch.

similar effect can be obtained by grasping a handful of the skin at the side of the neck and twisting, which is known as the 'neck twitch'.

Sedatives are occasionally used when treating difficult horses but are rarely recommended.

Two other problems which you might encounter are biting and kicking. A horse who has been accustomed to too many titbits will learn to bite when they are refused and a horse who is irritated, for example by the girth being tightened, may make as if to bite. Colts and stallions are more prone to biting than other horses. The answer is to avoid giving such horses an excuse to bite, as far as possible. For example, tighten your girth gently, being careful not to pinch the skin, and do not fuss too much around the horse's head — stroke his neck instead of his nose. When leading him, take a firm hold of the lead rope or reins close to his head so that he does not get the chance to bite your hand. If your horse does bite, reprimand him sharply. Hitting the horse on the nose is frequently used to try to prevent biting, but this is unlikely to work and may make the horse head-shy. Never hit a horse on his head, as he will soon learn to throw his head up out of your way every time you approach him.

Kicking should be dealt with as firmly as biting. However, few horses kick unless they are startled by something approaching suddenly from behind. Never approach your horse from the rear and if you move round to his rear end, speak to him and run your hand over his rump to let him know you are there. There is nothing vicious about a horse kicking out in fear, nor about the fit horse who may kick back a leg in nervous tension, for example, whilst being saddled up. A horse who continually kicks out at other horses, humans or dogs, however, for no apparent reason, must be taught not to do so. If possible, catch the horse as he kicks out, smacking him hard on the quarters (make sure you are out of the way of his kick) and saying loudly 'No'. Usually the habit can be cured by repeating this reprimand every time the horse kicks. If you take a known kicker out in company, you should put a red ribbon on his tail to warn other riders. (A young, green horse who might possibly kick should have a green ribbon.)

9 . Stable Equipment

When you buy your first horse, you will find you also have a seemingly endless shopping list of essential equipment. In this chapter we will look at different types of stable equipment and horse clothing and work out what is really necessary and what might be classed as optional.

HEADCOLLAR AND LEAD ROPE

The first items you will need are a headcollar and a lead rope. The horse may arrive complete with his headcollar and other tack; check any equipment that you buy with the horse to see that it is sound, safe and in good condition. Leather is the material traditionally used to make saddlery and it has several advantages which make it ideal for the purpose:

1. It is strong, but not so strong that it will not break in an emergency, so it is also safe.
2. Properly cared for, it is soft and supple and will not chafe the horse's skin.
3. It has an attractive feel to it and, when clean and well fitted, looks good.

Its only disadvantage is that it does require constant care to keep it in good condition, unlike some of the man-made materials.

For that last reason, many people use nylon webbing headcollars, which are strong, require little care other than an occasional scrub, and are virtually indestructible. The headcollar is often the most neglected item of tack! However, a well cared for leather headcollar is a bonus in any horse's tack room. The headcollar should fit well, snugly behind the ears and under the cheeks, with enough room in the noseband to allow the horse to open his mouth. Some headcollars have adjustable nosebands, which is useful if they are to be used for different horses.

The lead rope attaches to the ring of the headcollar under the horse's chin. Various types of spring clip are used and it is important to make sure that the side of the clip which opens is away from the horse's skin, to avoid any risk of the skin being caught and pinched. This should be remembered whenever spring clips are used on horse equipment, for example on side reins or on the leg straps of New Zealand rugs.

The rope itself should be thick enough to be held comfortably and will preferably be of natural fibre rope or webbing rather than nylon.

RUGS

Rugs form a major part of the expenditure on horse clothing and probably require repair or replacement more frequently than other items. A horse kept on the combined system of management will require a minimum of two rugs: a New Zealand (or turn-out) rug, plus a night rug (stable rug). Some 'multi-purpose' rugs are now available, which function as both. However, you will still need two rugs, as when one becomes soaked or needs cleaning or repair, the horse will need a spare.

Multi-purpose rugs usually come in man-made materials and the better ones allow the horse's skin to 'breath': they let sweat escape through the material, thus avoiding condensation and the chance of the horse becoming chilled underneath. They are usually lightweight and relatively strong.

Traditional New Zealand rugs — so named because that is where they originated — are made of heavy grade flax, or the cheaper variety of canvas. The latter become very heavy when wet and take a considerable time to dry out.

Night rugs are traditionally made of jute, although there are many man-made variations

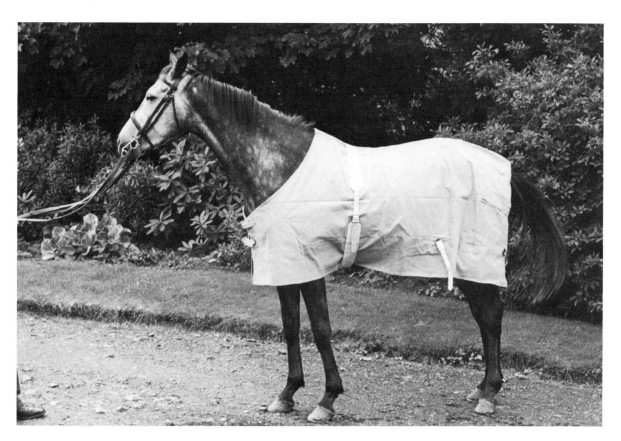

Fig 63   An inexpensive canvas New Zealand rug with a surcingle.

available, incorporating various stages of insulation technology. The best lining for traditional types of rug is wool. However, linings are also made from mixtures and man-made fibres. The determining factor is cost, so the better quality rugs are more likely to have wool, or predominantly wool, linings.

Rug fastenings vary considerably. Cheaper New Zealand rugs will have straps of leather (nylon webbing in the cheapest), chrome buckles and a detachable or sewn-in roller, which fastens around the girth. Other fastenings will be at the chest, usually with two buckles and with hind leg straps, which should be linked when fitted to help keep the rug in place. The possible disadvantage of a roller is that it may press on the horse's spine and cause discomfort or a sore. An alternative and increasingly popular type of fastening is the American crossed surcingle method, where two straps run from the front to the rear of the rug, crossing under the horse's belly. With this method, leg straps may or may not also be fitted and of course there will be front buckles at the chest.

The most important point to remember regarding rugs is that they must fit correctly. At any point where the rug is too tight, chafing will result. The most common points where this happens are over the withers, in horses with high withers, and at the shoulder especially if the horse has a long, sloping shoulder. Some rugs are shaped to fit, but be sure that the shaping of a particular rug fits your particular horse.

Once fitted, a rug will tend to slip backwards during the time the horse is wearing it, so rugs should be removed and refitted twice a day, to

85

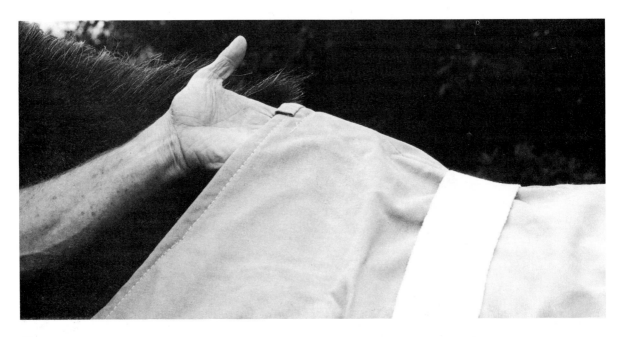

(a)

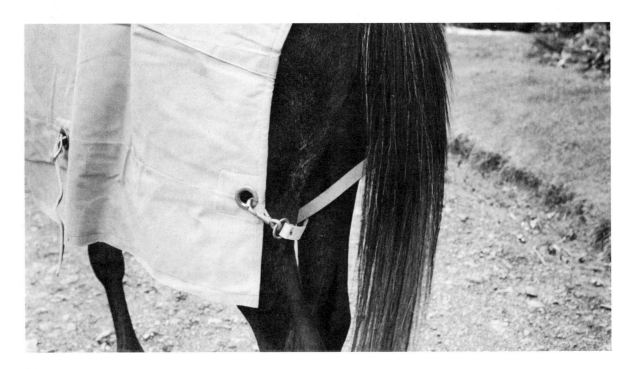

(b)

Fig 64 When fitting a rug, be sure that (a) it will not rub at the withers and
(b) the leg straps are adjusted correctly.

ensure the horse's comfort and avoid rubbing. When putting a rug on your horse, fold it from front to back and place it well forward on the horse. Unfold the front end towards the neck and slide the rug back into place, so that the horse's coat is lying flat, in the right direction. Never pull a rug forward into place. The accepted method of fastening a rug is to do up the roller, or girth fastenings, first, so that if a horse should be startled he will not end up with the rug hanging around his neck or around his hind legs. Then do up the chest straps and finally the leg straps. When removing the rug, reverse the procedure.

If you are planning to compete or take your horse to shows, you will also need some of the following rugs.

Anti-sweat Rug

This is the familiar 'string vest'. It is used underneath another rug or blanket, so that the spaces in the material, covered by another layer, trap air, which warms and helps to dry the horse. Using an anti-sweat rug on its own has no purpose whatsoever.

If you want to dry a sweating horse whilst also keeping him warm, thatching him with straw is a proven method. Your anti-sweat rug can be useful to keep the straw in place over his back and around his quarters, the whole then being covered by a stable rug or blanket. The heat built up by this method is considerable, so never leave a horse thatched for more than about one hour.

Fig 65 To help dry a sweating horse off quickly, he can be thatched with straw under his rug. Here an anti-sweat rug is used, covered with a day rug, quartered back and held in place by a roller.

Cooler

This is an all-in-one variation on the anti-sweat rug, to be used on its own on hot days. Coolers are usually made of stretch cotton, although the best kind, which can be used on colder days, are of fine wool. Ideally, a cooler will reach up to a horse's ears, thus also helping dry his neck and guard against chill.

Day Rug (Travelling Rug)

This is usually made of wool melton and is used, as its name implies, to keep the horse warm whilst travelling, usually over an anti-sweat rug. It can also be used under jute stable rugs for extra warmth. It is an optional item, unless you want your horse to look especially smart, as it can be replaced by blankets or stable rugs according to use. The classiest ones are sold with matching rollers and fillet strings. (A fillet string fits at the back of a rug, behind the hind legs and under the tail, to prevent the rug from blowing in the wind.)

Summer Sheet

This is principally used to protect the horse from pestering flies and to keep him clean whilst travelling to shows in hot weather. It is usually made of cotton and for this purpose is interchangeable with cotton coolers.

Rain Sheet

This is a waterproof sheet which comes up to the horse's ears and is designed to keep him and his tack dry whilst waiting to compete at shows or events. A very useful optional item!

Thermal Under-rug

Made of various man-made materials, using modern insulation technology, this rug is useful for competing horses who have to wait between competitions and as an under-rug, instead of a blanket, for clipped horses in winter.

Blanket

This is useful in many situations: for extra warmth under a stable rug, as a cooler or as a saddle pad or exercise sheet. The fact that it can be folded makes it adaptable and thus doubly useful. Various kinds are available, the best being pure wool.

To fit a blanket under a rug, put the folded blanket on, well up the horse's neck, unfold it and slide it back into position, leaving plenty at the front to fold back over the rug. Take the bottom front corner at each side and fold up over the horse's neck. Put the rug on, making sure that the blanket lies flat underneath. Fold the front, pointed fold of blanket back over the rug, beyond the withers so that it will be fastened under the roller. Do up the roller and the rug. In this way, several blankets can be used under one rug if required.

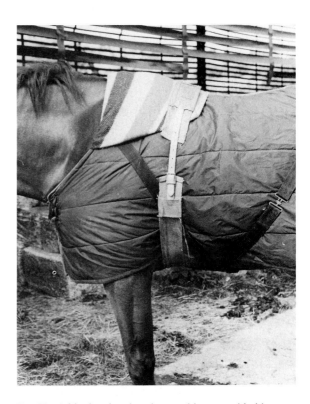

Fig 66 A blanket fitted under a stable rug and held in place by the roller.

STABLE AND TRAVELLING BANDAGES

At some time your horse may need stable bandages. The purpose of stable bandages is to provide warmth for tired legs, and to prevent filling and the development of minor swellings, such as wind-galls. However, their use is not advised unless it is really necessary and certainly not as a matter of course. Fitting stable bandages requires some skill, to prevent uneven pressure, and badly fitted bandages can cause more harm than they prevent. In the past 'cold water' bandages were often used when a horse came in from hard work, that is, gamgee soaked in cold water was placed under the stable bandages. However, the soaked gamgee soon becomes warm making the bandage ineffective. Ice packs and cold hosing are more useful.

Stable bandages, however, are also used for protection when travelling a horse, so it is a good idea to spend some time learning how to bandage correctly. Travelling bandages should extend

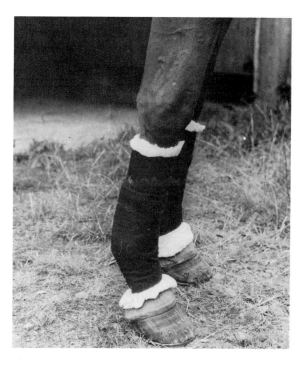

Fig 68 The stable bandage continues down over the fetlock joint and half-way back up the cannon bone. The tapes are tied neatly on the outside of the leg, with a fold of bandage turned down to secure them.

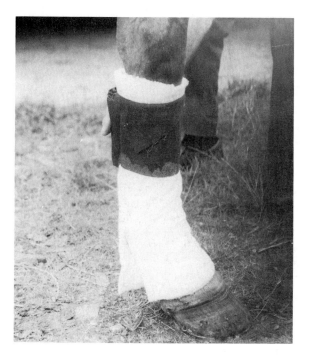

Fig 67 Fitting a stable bandage, near foreleg.

from just below the knee to the coronet. Start at the top and always bandage over gamgee or similar leg padding, to even out the pressure. Always bandage from the inside of the leg, around the front to the outside, so that if the bandage comes undone, there is less chance of the horse tripping over it. Hold the end of the bandage against the leg and take a turn or two to secure it. Turn down the loose end and bandage over it so that it is neatly tucked out of the way. Continue bandaging down the leg, covering half the width of the previous bandage turn each time. Bandage closely around the fetlock, leaving the padding protruding below the bandage to protect the heels and coronet, then bandage back up the leg to the end of the bandage. The bandage should be firm, but not so tight that it is impossible to slide two fingers between the bandage and the leg. Tie the tapes no tighter than the bandage, fastening them in a bow on the outside of the leg, where the knot will not press on the cannon bone or tendons. Turn a fold of bandage down over the bow and tuck the tapes out of sight. When removing a bandage, do so quickly, passing the bandage from hand to hand; do not try to re-roll the bandage as you go.

Another bandage that you will use in the stable or travelling is the tail bandage. Its purpose is to protect the tail from rubbing and to improve the appearance of the tail by helping the hair to lie flat. A tail bandage may have lint on one side to improve its grip. If the horse dislikes having his tail bandaged get someone to help you and place a stable door, or some straw bales, between the horse and yourself to avoid being kicked. Lift the dock and take two turns around the tail near the top with your bandage; then, once the bandage is secure, take two or three more turns to cover the highest part of the dock. Continue bandaging to just above the end of the dock, then back upwards to the end of the

bandage, approximately half-way up the dock. Tie the tapes on top of the tail, not at the sides or underneath where they might rub, then turn a fold of bandage down over the tapes. To remove a tail bandage, grasp it from the top and slide down over the tail.

OTHER TRAVELLING PROTECTION

Protection from knocks, bumps and rubs is the most important aspect of a horse's travelling kit, and other items to be included are a tail guard, hock and knee boots and a poll guard.

The tail guard can be used on its own or over a tail bandage. The best ones are made of leather, although good tail guards are available in various synthetic materials. Felt or melton tail guards are subject to wear if the horse likes to lean back on the ramp or side of the vehicle.

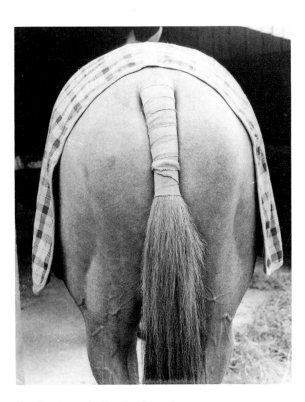

Fig 69   A neatly fitted tail bandage.

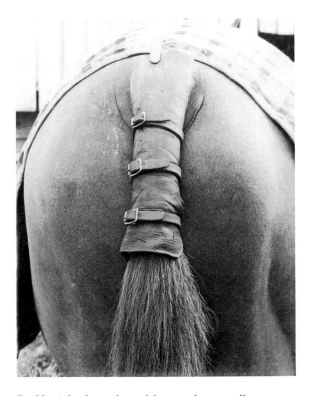

Fig 70   A leather tail guard for use when travelling.

90

Hock and knee boots are essential to prevent damage to these vital joints. They may be made of wool and leather or felt, with leather straps and buckles, or the synthetic 'touch and close' type of fastening. They should be fastened snugly above the joint, but the lower straps should be slack to allow the horse plenty of room for movement.

If you do not want to use bandages for travelling your horse, there are specially made travelling boots available, from leather and sheepskin-lined boots to those with nylon fabric outers and acrylic fleece linings. Some travelling boots extend above the hock and knee to incorporate joint protection. The main thing to ensure is that the boots will remain in place without slipping down during the journey.

A poll guard is designed to protect the top of the horse's head, should he throw it up and hit it on the top of the trailer or horse-box. It fits on to his headcollar and over his poll, with holes for his ears and is usually made of leather, thickly lined with felt.

This completes the list of your horse's stable and travelling equipment, but there are several other items that you will need to provide for his daily care.

OTHER EQUIPMENT

At least three buckets will be needed, for water, mixing feed and for miscellaneous uses such as washing equipment or bathing the horse. Ideally, keep separate buckets for each use, so that feed and water buckets do not become contaminated by shampoo or soap powder.

The best way to feed hay is in a hay-net and two of these will give you a spare for travelling or in case one breaks. Hay-nets should be hung so that when empty they will not dangle within reach of the horse's feet, where he could become caught up. Pull the draw-string through the tie-ring, then through the mesh near the bottom of the hay-net. Pull it up as tightly as you can, then tie it with a

Fig 71   Royal Fun, ready to travel in anti-sweat rug and day rug, tail bandage under the tail guard and all-in-one travelling boots.

quick release knot. Pass the end of the draw-string through the loop of the knot to prevent the horse from undoing it.

Your horse's equipment will last much longer if you take good care of it. Leather items should be cleaned regularly and treated with a leather preservative. Wool and felt items should be brushed thoroughly to remove dirt and hairs and put out to air. Cotton rugs, coolers and woollen blankets and bandages can be washed, in soap-flakes, or animal shampoo, not in detergent, which could cause skin problems. Always rinse thoroughly, then hang them up to dry. Some rugs can be machine-washed — follow the manufacturer's instructions. Flax, canvas and jute rugs can be brushed or scrubbed as appropriate, and the linings brushed clean. Grooming brushes should also be washed regularly, in medicated animal shampoo.

An important part of your stable equipment should be an emergency equine first aid kit. This should contain:

1. Antiseptic or antibiotic wound dressing or powder.
2. Cotton wool.
3. Three or four elastic bandages, approximately 4in (10cm) wide.
4. Small supply of gauze dressings.
5. Poultice dressing.
6. Safety pins and scissors.
7. Proprietary hock and knee bandages

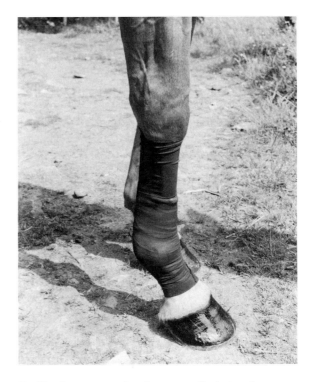

Fig 72 A proprietary bandage, specially designed to cover the fetlock joint.

(optional); these are useful, as these joints are difficult to bandage, but they are expensive.

The final essential, a grooming kit, will be considered in detail in Chapter 12.

10 . Riding Equipment

SADDLES

Your major item of expenditure in terms of riding equipment will be your saddle. A good saddle, properly cared for, will last a lifetime and saddles become as individual as their owners and the horses who wear them. Choosing a saddle from scratch is a difficult task as it must both fit your horse well, and be comfortable for you to ride in. Better makes of saddles come in three fittings, narrow, medium and wide, although you can also have your saddle custom-made for your horse, if your budget will stretch to this.

Apart from the width fitting, saddles vary in type according to the purpose for which they are to be used: dressage, showjumping, eventing,

showing, endurance riding, western riding or side saddle. As most riders wish to use one saddle for several different purposes, the most commonly used saddle is the general-purpose saddle. This is a compromise between the dressage and jumping saddles, having a deeper seat than a jumping saddle, but being forward cut, with knee rolls which help keep the rider in the saddle when jumping.

Another compromise saddle is the combination eventing saddle, which is forward cut with knee rolls for jumping, but has a deep dressage seat and recessed stirrup bars. This type of saddle may also have long girth straps to enable a dressage girth to be used, giving the rider closer contact with the horse by avoiding having the girth buckles under the leg.

The pure dressage saddle has a deep seat and is designed for the closest possible contact with the horse. The flap is straight cut, as the rider's position necessitates a long, straight leg so that the shoulder of the horse can be shown off to the full.

The jumping saddle has a shallower seat and a less high cantle, enabling the rider's seat to slide back when he folds his body over a fence. The shorter stirrup length necessitates a forward cut flap to accommodate the rider's knee, with knee rolls and sometimes thigh rolls, for added stability.

The show saddle is smaller and lighter than competition saddles, designed to cover as little of the horse as possible, whilst still affording a comfortable seat to the rider and judge.

The traditional English hunting saddle would be considered uncomfortable by many riders today, having a flattish seat and lacking knee rolls. The western saddle, with its high pommel and cantle and armchair-like seat is the opposite, being almost impossible to fall out of. It has much in common with the military saddle, both being

Fig 73   A custom-made event saddle, with deep seat, recessed stirrup bars and forward cut flaps.

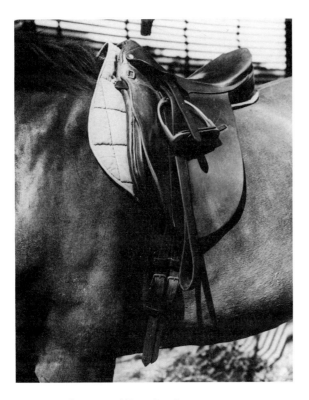

Fig 74   A dressage saddle and girth, worn over a general-purpose numnah to demonstrate the straight cut flap.

designed for riders who spend long hours in the saddle. Many lightweight endurance saddles are built on the same principle.

Fitting

Your first purchase is likely to be a general-purpose riding-horse saddle, and the only way to be sure that it will be satisfactory is to have your saddler fit it to your horse, and to sit in it to see if it is comfortable for yourself. To fit the rider, the saddle should have a seat of the correct size. A 17in (42.5cm) seat is about average, but seat sizes commonly vary between 16in (40cm) and 18in (45cm), so check what is most comfortable. The flap must be long enough not to catch the top of your boot, but not so long that it impedes your leg aids.

A saddle that does not fit your horse is a recipe

for back problems and poor performance; it should fit correctly without the addition of a numnah. You may wish to use a numnah to provide extra protection and cushioning but it will not compensate for the pressure of a badly fitting saddle. The saddle should sit comfortably on the horse's back, just behind the withers, and should not be so long in the seat that it causes pressure on the loins. There should be a clear channel above the horse's spine along the gullet of the saddle – you should be able to see daylight through this space – to ensure that the saddle does not press on the spine. Check this mounted as well as dismounted.

When putting on your horse's saddle, lower it gently, well forward of the withers and slide it back into position, so that the hair lies flat underneath and is not rubbed the wrong way. The girth should be attached to the two front straps (the third is a spare for use in an emergency), with the buckle guards positioned over the buckles to protect the saddle flap. Do up the girth by degrees and remember to check it before you mount. Before mounting, you can pull each of the horse's forelegs forward in turn, to ensure that the skin is not being pinched under the girth.

Saddle Components

If you buy a new saddle, it should be in good condition, but if you buy second hand, be sure to have the tree checked. A broken or twisted tree can damage your horse's back. The tree is the framework on which the saddle is built, usually made of laminated beechwood, but possibly of fibreglass in modern saddles. The tree can be either rigid or sprung, the latter being the most popular for riding horses today as the slight give in the seat makes the saddle more comfortable for the rider. However, a spring tree does result in a little more friction on the horse's back and some endurance riders prefer to use a rigid tree for this reason. The 'spring' is achieved by the use of two metal strips running from front to back on either side of the tree.

The stuffing and lining of the saddle should be

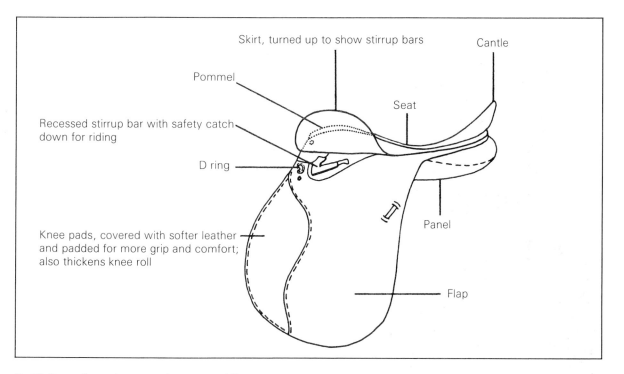

Fig 75 Parts of a modern general-purpose saddle (side view).

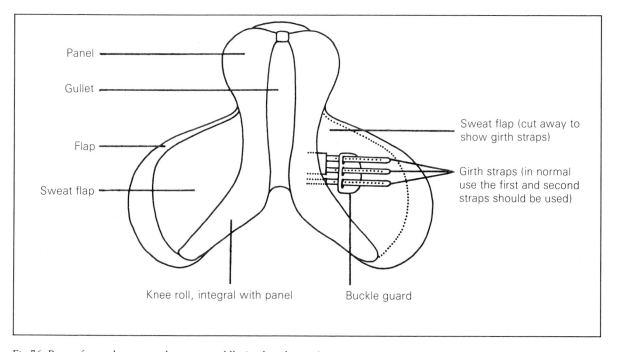

Fig 76 Parts of a modern general-purpose saddle (underside view).

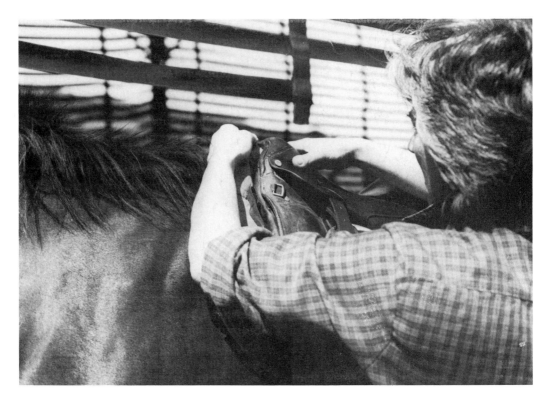

Fig 77   When saddling up, be sure to pull the numnah well up into the channel
to avoid pressure on the horse's back.

smooth and even, with the stuffing equal on both sides. Wool is the traditional material used for stuffing saddles and has the advantage of moulding itself to the horse's back, but synthetic materials are frequently used nowadays. In fact, saddle manufacture remained unchanged for many years, but with the advent of modern technology, new ideas are appearing on the market each year. Linings are usually made of leather today, although in the past serge and linen were often used. Leather has the advantage of being durable and easy to clean.

With your saddle you will need stirrup irons and leathers, girths, probably a minimum of two numnahs or saddle pads and, as an optional extra, a seat cover. A saddle cover is also useful to protect your saddle if you are regularly transporting it to shows and events.

Stirrup Irons and Leathers

Stirrup irons, like bits, used to be made of nickel but nowadays are usually of stainless steel. They may have metal treads or rubber safety treads, and should be large enough for your foot to slip out easily should you fall off. Children's safety stirrups have a gap in the metal on the outside, which is closed by a strong rubber band that springs off under pressure from the foot.

Stirrup leathers come in various lengths and qualities, some of which stretch more than others, so buy the best quality you can afford.

Girths

There are several types of girth in common use, the most popular general-purpose girth being the foam-padded type, which is less inclined to rub. Leather girths are durable and good for fit horses, but must be kept in very good condition to avoid rubbing. Leather girths include the Balding and Atherstone girths, which are shaped behind the elbows, and the three-fold girth. Lampwick girths, made of soft, tubular webbing, are good for horses in soft condition. Nylon string girths are widely used for ponies but are unsuitable for thinner-skinned horses.

Numnahs and Seat Covers

Numnahs, or saddle pads, can vary from the best sheepskin, to folded wool blankets, to one of the many acrylic fleece or quilted cotton varieties available. Their purpose is to provide cushioning under the saddle, to reduce jarring, especially when jumping, or when the rider is in the saddle for a long period of time. Natural fibres are preferable, as they are more absorbent, but those made of modern surgical materials are also good. Avoid a thin saddle cloth that may wrinkle and cause pressure bumps.

Seat covers are designed for the comfort of the rider and may be of sheepskin or acrylic fleece.

BRIDLES

The other major item of tack you will require is a bridle. If you do not buy the bridle with your horse, be sure to find out what bit he is accustomed to wearing, as a sudden change of bit may completely alter his way of going.

Snaffles

The most commonly used bit is the snaffle. This may be a straight bar, mullen mouthed (a slightly curved bar, which is a very mild bit), single-jointed or double-jointed. There are also many much more severe variations on the snaffle, such as the twisted snaffle, or the wire snaffle, and these are to be avoided.

The bit's thickness may vary, the general principle being the thicker the bit, the milder its action. The bit may have loose rings or fixed rings, as in the eggbut. Fixed rings give a more precise and direct action from the rider's hand to the horse's mouth. The mouthpiece itself may be of rubber (in the mildest bits), vulcanite, nylon or stainless steel.

The snaffle bit acts upon the corners of the lips, the tongue and the bars of the horse's mouth (the area between the incisors at the front and the molars at the back of the mouth). It has a 'nutcracker' or squeezing action, which raises the horse's head. In the double-jointed versions, the nutcracker action is reduced, while the pressure on the bars of the mouth is slightly increased. There are two double-jointed snaffles in common use, the French snaffle, which has a flat link and is a mild bit, especially useful for young or unschooled horses, and the Dr Bristol, which has the link set edgewise, so that it presses on the tongue and is much more severe. The two look very similar and should not be confused.

The gag is a strong form of snaffle, usually used for pulling hunters. The rein is attached to the cheek-pieces of the bridle through spaces in the bit rings, so that when the reins are taken up, pressure is exerted strongly on the poll as well as on the mouth. It is a severe bit, and should not be used by inexperienced riders.

Pelhams

The second type of bit you are likely to encounter in common use is the pelham. This bit combines the action of a snaffle with that of a curb bit, which exerts pressure on the poll and the jaw. A pelham can only be used correctly with two reins and must be used with light hands to be effective without restricting the horse's neck. Unfortunately, the misuse of the pelham as a means of stopping horses who pull, usually with a single rein and 'roundings', has given it an undeserved bad reputation.

The pelham is frequently useful for show horses whose mouths are too small to accommodate a double bridle comfortably. As with the snaffle, pelhams come with mouthpieces of varying designs, but mullen mouthed vulcanite is the most commonly used version.

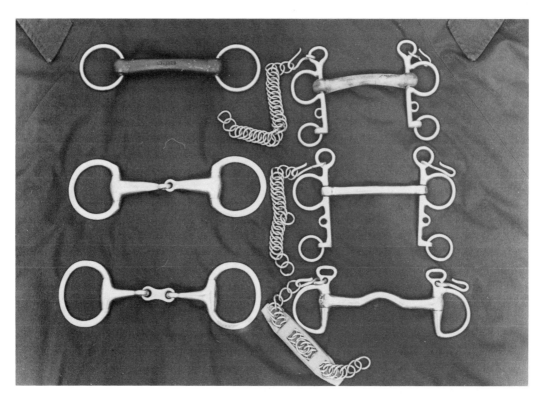

Fig 78 Bits in common use (from top left): vulcanite mullen mouth snaffle; jointed eggbut snaffle; French snaffle. (Right): vulcanite pelham; stainless steel mullen mouth pelham; kimblewick (frequently used for strong ponies).

Double Bridles

The double bridle has two bits, the snaffle bit, known as the bridoon, and the curb bit, each having an independent action enabling the skilled rider to give precise aids. The severity of a curb bit, apart from the actions of the rider, depends upon the design of the mouthpiece, the length of the cheeks and the tightness of the curb chain. The mouthpiece may be the mullen type, or it may have a 'port' or arch. The higher the port, the stronger the bit may be, and a port that touches the roof of the horse's mouth can cause considerable pain and should not be used.

Shorter cheeks are less severe than long ones, because of the degree of leverage employed. A curb chain should be adjusted so that it does not come into action until the cheek-pieces reach an angle of 45 degrees from the horse's mouth.

Double bridles are usually used for show horses, advanced dressage horses and occasionally for hunters or event horses.

Bridle Components

The straightforward snaffle bridle comprises a head-piece, including the throat-latch which prevents the bridle falling off, browband, cheek-pieces, noseband and reins. The double bridle has, in addition, a slip-head — a thin strap which slots through the ends of the browband — plus a cheek-piece, to which the bridoon is attached.

Bridle leather may be of varying widths according to the purpose for which it is required. For example, show bridles are usually of material thinner in width to show off the horse's head, and may be decorated with fancy stitching, whereas a hunter bridle needs to be more robust.

Fig 79   This horse, preparing for the dressage phase in a one-day event, is wearing a double bridle and dressage saddle.

Fig 80   The same horse, now in the cross-country phase, wears a snaffle bit with cheek-pieces, a running martingale and a forward cut saddle. The rider has changed her jacket and velvet cap for a jersey, crash hat and silk.

Nosebands vary in design, according to their purpose, the standard noseband being the straightforward cavesson. Its function is basically to improve the horse's appearance when bridled, although if fitted fairly tightly it may go some way towards discouraging the horse from opening his mouth.

The next most frequently used noseband is the dropped noseband, which has a fixed nose-piece, with the bottom strap going underneath the bit. It should only be used with a snaffle bit and its purpose is to reinforce the action of the bit by acting on the nose to lower the head carriage, so that the bit sits correctly in the mouth and can be used effectively. It is also useful in preventing a horse from getting his tongue over the bit if he is so inclined, and from opening his mouth.

The flash noseband is a cavesson with a dropped noseband attached. It does not exert the pressure of the dropped noseband on the nose,

Fig 82   A flash noseband.

but prevents the horse from opening his mouth and crossing his jaw.

The grakle is a crossed noseband, with one strap fastening above the bit, the other beneath it. It restricts the breathing less than a dropped noseband and is fastened slightly higher. It has a similar effect, but allows the horse to move his jaw whilst exerting stronger pressure where the straps cross over the nose. It is often used for galloping horses such as eventers or steeplechasers.

The kineton noseband has two metal loops which pass from the cheeks, under the bit to the nose-piece, thus transferring the pressure from the bit to the nose. It is used for hard-pulling horses.

Fitting

To put on a bridle, put the reins over the horse's head and remove the headcollar. Standing at the

Fit 81   A correctly fitted drop noseband, with a snaffle bit.

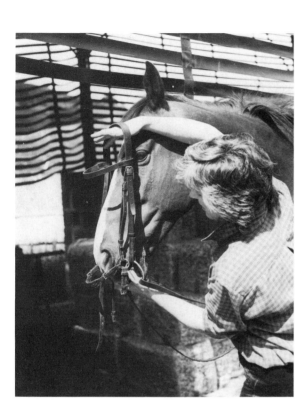

Fig 83   Another way of fitting a bridle.

left side of the horse, take the cheek-pieces of the bridle in your right hand, holding the noseband out of the way of the bit. Pass this hand, with the bridle, under the horse's chin, around the far side of his head and over his nose. Raise the bit to his mouth in your left palm and if the horse does not open his mouth, slide your thumb into his mouth, between the bars, to encourage him to open it. Slip the bit into his mouth and move your left hand up to guide the head-piece gently over his ears. Take care not to rub the bridle against his eyes. Do up the throat-latch, then the noseband and finally, if applicable, the curb chain. Reverse the process when removing the bridle, taking care not to bang the bit against the horse's teeth.

OTHER TACK

Other items of tack which you may require at some time or other include martingales, cruppers, breastplates and surcingles.

The running martingale is useful for young horses and whenever you want to prevent a horse from raising his head to evade the bit. It is often used for hunting, jumping and cross-country riding for this purpose. It comprises a strap from the girth, which divides into two at the chest, each ending in a ring through which a rein is passed. It is supported by a neck strap; rubber stops are needed on the reins to stop the rings sliding up and interfering with the bit, and at the chest to prevent the chest strap sliding down from the neck strap.

A standing martingale attaches to the noseband instead of the reins and also prevents a horse from raising his head, but restricts the movement of the head and neck if jumping, so is less useful than a running martingale.

The Market Harborough is similar to a running martingale, except that in place of rings it has longer straps which pass through the bit rings and hook to specially fitted Ds on the reins. It acts directly on the bit when the horse raises his head, rather than on the reins, and is a useful schooling device, especially for young horses.

A crupper is a strap which runs from the back of the saddle around and under the dock. Its purpose is to prevent the saddle slipping forward and it is useful for ponies with rotund conformation and low withers.

The purpose of a breastplate is to prevent the saddle slipping back on horses with high withers, or narrow guts, or when jumping, hunting or crossing hilly ground. The most commonly used type is the hunting breastplate, which has a strap from the girth to a neck strap, in which there are rings either side of the withers. These are for the attachment of further straps from the D rings at the front of the saddle. Frequently, a running martingale attachment is also supplied.

TACK CARE

The quality of leather varies tremendously and it will always pay to buy the best you can afford. Leathers from all over the world are used in saddle making; in general the leather should feel thick and supple, with a dense, slightly greasy texture. Cowhide is used for basic saddlery work, but many saddles have pigskin or doeskin seats, with doeskin or suede-covered knee rolls, which give more grip, but wear less well.

It is all too easy to neglect caring for your tack, when you come in tired or wet from a ride and the television or a cup of tea beckons. The best thing to do is to make a basic rule and stick to it. There is no need to dismantle all your tack to clean it every day after use. If you make a point of doing so once a week, you can simply give it a rub over to remove mud and sweat on the other days.

To clean your tack thoroughly, take it apart and wash and dry the bit and stirrup irons (drying them will prevent rust spots, even on stainless steel). Using a damp sponge, wash the leather pieces clean of mud, sweat, grease and marks from the bit and irons. Pay particular attention to the buckle tabs, especially where the bit and irons lie on the leather. With an almost dry sponge, rub plenty of glycerine saddle soap into the leather, again paying attention to the buckle tabs and anywhere subject to pressure. Leave for a short time, then polish with a soft cloth.

Once a month (more often if it gets very wet and muddy), waterproof your tack by going over it with a proprietary waterproof dressing or oil. The flesh side of the leather will absorb more oil than the hair side. Oiling is particularly important for new saddles, which may squeak annoyingly unless well lubricated. Be sure to oil all the underneath parts of the flaps and the skirt well. Do not oil the seat of your saddle as the oil will not penetrate this side of the leather and will come off on your breeches or riding trousers.

If it is too much of a chore to use traditional saddle soap there are various specially formulated leather preservatives which are gaining in popularity. The important thing is to keep your leather tack supple and strong. Never let it dry out as this will weaken the leather and lead to breakages. If it becomes soaked in bad weather, hang it up to dry naturally; do not put it near a source of direct heat as, again, this will lead to too rapid drying and will weaken the leather. New tack needs oiling more frequently than used tack for this reason. In fact, new leather tack needs to be broken in rather like a new pair of shoes, and experienced riders would much rather use an old familiar saddle than a pristine new one.

Modern technology has produced bridles and ancillary pieces of tack made of strong nylon webbing as an alternative to leather and these are extremely practical for everyday use, only needing to be scrubbed under a tap or even put into the washing machine when dirty. The better makes have built-in breakage points for safety, and care has been taken in the design to see that they do not rub the horse's skin. However, they do not have the traditionally attractive appearance of leather in the show ring or competition arena.

11 . Exercise, Schooling and Competition Equipment

As your experience of riding and horse ownership progresses, you will find there are other items of equipment you need. You will want to take your horse to shows, school him at home and there will be days when you cannot ride him for some reason but he will still need exercise. In this case, lungeing is the answer.

LUNGEING

Lungeing a horse correctly and effectively is an art not to be learned from a book, but it is a useful

Fig 84 The lungeing cavesson, fitted over a snaffle bridle, with the reins looped round the horse's neck and fastened through the throat-latch to keep them out of the way, and side reins fitted.

skill for any horse owner to have, and if you don't know how to do it correctly, ask an experienced person to show you, or have some lessons. All horses benefit from being lunged occasionally, as it gives them the opportunity to work in a controlled outline without the imposition of a rider, so the muscles can be really stretched and balance and suppleness improved. Lungeing plays a major part in ensuring the correct outline and muscle development of young horses in the early stages of their training.

A horse can be lunged from the bridle, but this should not be attempted until some experience of lungeing has been gained. Instead, a lungeing cavesson is used — a strong headcollar of leather or nylon webbing, which has a padded noseband with three metal rings attached. This is fitted to the horse on its own or over a bridle, the noseband preferably being fastened under the cheek-pieces of the bridle. The lunge rein can be made of webbing or nylon and should be about 20ft (6m) long. It is attached by means of a swivel clip to the centre ring of the cavesson (the other two rings are usually used for longreining).

A lunge whip is needed to guide the horse and encourage him forward if necessary. The lighter-weight whips are preferable as they are easier to use, being less tiring on the wrist. The lunge whip must always be used with extreme tact and the trainer must be careful never to frighten the horse with it.

Side reins may be used, once a horse has been taught to lunge correctly, to encourage the horse to reach for and accept the bit, and to achieve the correct head carriage. Like all artificial schooling aids, they should not be used by the inexperienced owner who has not been taught how to use them, as more harm will be done than

Fig 85 For lungeing, the stirrup leathers are plaited through the irons to prevent them slipping down and the horse wears brushing boots, to protect him from injury.

good. Side reins are attached to the girth straps at one end, or to a roller with rings suitably positioned, and to the bit at the other end. They may be of plain leather, or, more commonly nowadays, of leather with a rubber or elastic insert to allow some give in the reins when the horse moves his head.

Finally, to prevent the possibility of the horse injuring himself, he should wear exercise bandages or boots. Boots are easier to put on and various types are available. They may be made of leather or synthetic materials and may fasten with straps and buckles or 'touch and close' fastenings. Their function is to protect the lower leg, especially the tendons, from injury (due to brushing or the horse striking into himself) and to provide some support.

EXERCISING AND SCHOOLING

Bandages provide more support than most boots and are preferable for young horses whose legs have not yet hardened off. Exercise bandages are fitted from just below the knee to just above the fetlock, unlike stable bandages which continue down to the coronet. However, the same principles of bandaging apply and it is particularly important to apply the bandages smoothly and to avoid uneven pressure. Exercise bandages are elasticated to prevent slipping and provide extra support, but they must not be fitted so tightly that the circulation to the leg is restricted. You should be able to slide two fingers under the bandage after it has been put on. Remember always to bandage clockwise on the off-side (right) legs and anticlockwise on the near-side (left) legs. Exercise bandages should always be fitted over gamgee.

Fig 86 Exercise bandages must be neatly and smoothly applied, with the tapes tied on the outside.

Fig 87 Correctly fitted exercise bandages. It should be possible to slide two fingers under the bandages, to ensure that they are not too tight.

Schooling exercises require the horse to move his hind legs strongly underneath himself and often one across in front of the other. He will be continuously bending and changing direction, so the risk of injury is greater than when out hacking. Therefore it is a good idea to protect your horse's legs whenever you are schooling him, whether he is being lunged or ridden.

Boots are available to protect all parts of the working horse's lower leg, depending upon the demands of the competition and the peculiarities of the individual horse's action. They include tendon boots, brushing boots of many designs, fetlock boots, polo boots and overreach boots. Polo boots extend down over the pastern and heel. Overreach boots are those bell-shaped boots, usually of rubber, used to protect the heels of the front feet from injury by the hind feet as they stretch forward, especially when the horse is being jumped.

When exercising your horse on the road, especially if he is a show horse, skeleton knee boots may be a sensible precaution. These are often also used for racehorses or competition horses, with riders becoming more aware of the increasing dangers of roadwork and the damage that can be caused to a horse's knees should he fall on them. Skeleton knee boots are usually made of leather and are similar to travelling knee boots, without the padding. They are fitted with a secure strap above the knee and with a loose strap below the knee, so that the horse is able to flex the joint. A variation on this design, with two straps above the knee, is available for jumping.

If your horse is kept stabled and clipped, an exercise sheet might be useful for exercising on cold days or whilst working in before a competition. These are usually of melton or wool and are fitted under the saddle, covering the horse's back and quarters to keep his muscles warm and avoid possible strain. Exercise sheets are also available in waterproof material for use in wet weather.

Other equipment that may be needed varies according to the use of the horse.

(a)

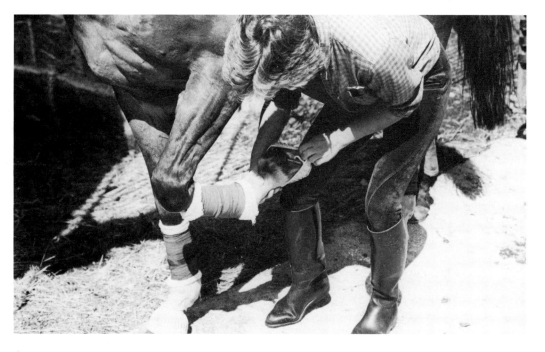

(b)

Fig 88 (a) Fitting and (b) removing overreach boots.

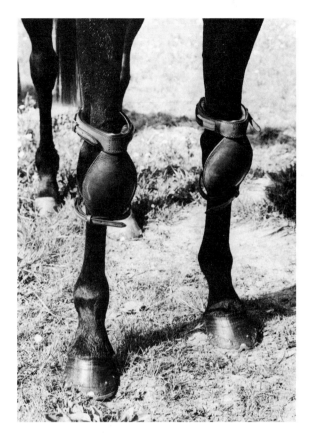

Fig 89 Skeleton knee boots – a sensible precaution for roadwork.

DRESSAGE

A snaffle (or for advanced competition, a double bridle) is required, together with a dressage saddle with dressage girth, or a general-purpose saddle if a dressage saddle is not available. Numnahs are usually worn and should be of the same design as the saddle. Protective boots and bandages are not worn in competition.

Rider's dress varies according to the level of the competition, from 'rat-catcher', that is, a tweed hacking jacket with collar and tie, to the elegant tailcoats worn in advanced competition. If you are unsure what to wear for any type of competition, check the rules of your club or society. For most novice level and riding club events in all disciplines, boots, breeches or jodhpurs, collar and tie, tweed jacket, gloves and hard hat conforming to current safety standards will be acceptable.

SHOWJUMPING

Basic tack will comprise a general-purpose or jumping saddle, snaffle bridle with cavesson or dropped noseband and probably a running martingale. The showjumper is required to manoeuvre in a comparatively confined space and many riders find a running martingale is useful to prevent the horse from getting above the bit and becoming unbalanced when approaching his fences. Professional showjumpers use many different bits and bridles, and fashions come and go, but stick to a simple mouthpiece if possible, or one in which you know your horse goes well. Remember that 'gadgets' will never compensate for good schooling.

Fairly thick numnahs are usually used, to reduce the likelihood of jarring the horse's back as the rider comes back into the saddle on landing, and a breastplate may be useful if your horse has the type of conformation which is inclined to allow the saddle to slip back. Breastplates and martingales must be carefully fitted to avoid restricting the horse's ability to stretch over his fences. Leg protection all round is a good idea when jumping, particularly to the tendons of the front legs, to prevent any risk from the horse striking into himself as he lands. Open-fronted tendon boots are popularly used. Overreach boots are also invariably used, for the same reason.

EVENTING

Equipment for the dressage and showjumping phases is as outlined above, although you may have a combination event saddle which can be used for all three phases of the competition.

For the cross-country phase you will need a saddle in which you can jump comfortably and in view of the strenuous nature of the exercise it is

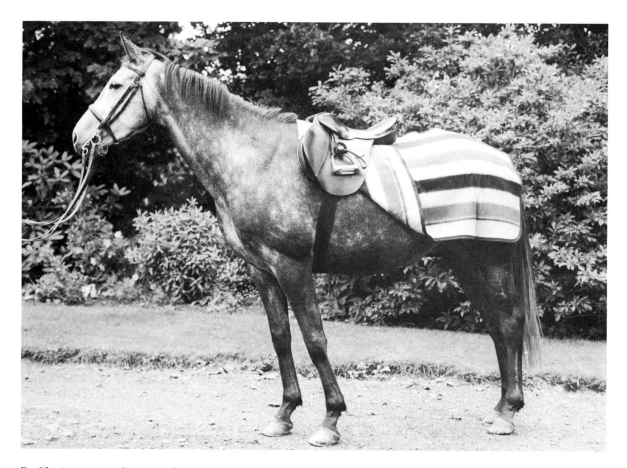

Fig 90　An exercise sheet − useful in cold weather.

advisable to put a surcingle on. This is a webbing strap, usually with an elastic insert, which fits over the top of the saddle and around the horse's girth. Its purpose is to avoid accidents should your girth break.

Leather reins are slippery if they get wet, from rain or sweat, and for jumping most riders prefer rubber-covered reins or the Continental-style webbing reins with stops.

As with showjumping, a breastplate is usually used, together with a running martingale. Grakle, flash or dropped nosebands are also often fitted to give greater control with a snaffle bit.

Leg protection is essential when jumping cross-country; brushing boots or bandages should be used. The fleece-lined type are excellent, although expensive. Leather brushing boots must be kept very supple and soft if chafing is to be avoided, whilst the rubber-lined type may also cause chafing, as they do not absorb sweat. There are also some very good synthetic boots available now, although they too tend to be expensive. Many people still prefer to use bandages, but they become heavy if waterlogged. If bandages are used, they should be taped to prevent them coming undone.

Overreach boots are optional − they may prevent injury from the horse striking into himself, but can become inverted in heavy going and the current tendency is not to use them for cross-country work.

In wet, muddy conditions, some people like to plait and tape up their horses' tails to prevent

Fig 91 Dressed for showjumping – the horse wears a jumping saddle, snaffle with flash noseband and running martingale, open-fronted tendon boots and overreach boots on his forelegs, and fetlock boots on his hind legs. The rider wears a velvet cap, black jacket, white breeches and black riding boots.

them becoming dirty and tangled. Finally, it is common practice to smear the front of the horse's legs liberally with grease before going across country, to minimise the effect of him knocking himself on the fixed fences.

Studs

For both showjumping and cross-country riding, studs are fitted to the horse's shoes to give more grip. Studs can be fixed but jumping studs are usually screwed in so that they can be removed when the horse is not jumping. Leaving large studs in all the time unbalances the horse's foot. Large, square studs are used for jumping on soft going, whilst sharper ones can be used for jumping off grass on hard ground.

Road studs are often fitted, to give extra grip if a lot of roadwork has to be done, but are best avoided if possible, again because of the unbalancing effect on the feet. If you want extra grip on the roads, tungsten nails are a better alternative – they have a hard tungsten centre which wears more slowly than the shoes. There is a theory that the small amount of slip that occurs

Fig 92 Dressed for cross-country work – the horse wears a gag snaffle, flash noseband and running martingale, with a surcingle over the saddle. He also has taped bandages over leg protectors. The rider wears a skull cap with silk, gloves and spurs and has a back protector under her jersey, hence the bulky look.

109

each time the horse puts down a foot helps to prevent concussion, so consider the situation carefully before you resort to anti-slipping devices, except for removable jumping studs.

ENDURANCE RIDING

Comfort, of both horse and rider, is the main criterion to consider when fitting out your endurance horse. The basic rule is to use the minimum of tack necessary, to avoid the chance of rubbing the skin during the long hours of wear. Make sure your saddle fits well, whether it is a specialist endurance saddle or a general-purpose type — sore backs caused by pressure from badly fitting saddles are a common problem.

Choose a numnah which will absorb sweat and will not crease under the saddle. Sheepskin, or the synthetic 'medical' fabrics, or a folded wool blanket seem to work best. If your saddle fits well

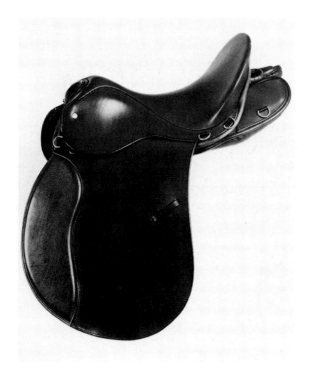

Fig 93 A specially designed endurance riding saddle, the Endurance LDR, by EPIC.

you should not need a breastplate except in really mountainous country, and many riders also dispense with the noseband.

Bruised mouths can attract penalties, so very keen horses are often ridden in hackamores rather than bits. The hackamore is a bitless bridle, which operates by exerting pressure on the horse's nose and under the jaw. It has a strong action and must be used with sympathetic hands.

Your bridle must be strong but light and various designs are available which can be converted for use as a headcollar at mandatory halts, by unbuckling the bit and fastening the lead rope to a ring in the noseband under the chin. Nylon webbing bridles are popular for endurance work in the United States but care must be taken to see that they do not rub. During a long ride you will need at least one change of numnah and girth. Leg protection may be worn for some competitions, but is usually avoided, as in a ride of 50 miles (80 kilometres) or more there is more danger from grit or mud getting inside the boots or bandages and causing a sore, than from the horse injuring himself with a knock.

HUNTING

A general-purpose saddle and a working bridle form the basis of hunting tack. Horses tend to become excited out hunting and riders resort to all kinds of bits for greater control. The gag snaffle is frequently used for strong horses who pull hard, whilst some riders prefer a double bridle. However, in the hunting field, as in any other equestrian sphere, a multitude of tack designed to keep the horse under control usually means a poorly schooled horse, so work on the principle of keeping your equipment simple but effective and learn how to use it correctly.

Numnahs were seldom used in the days when saddles were lined with serge or linen instead of leather, but now most people like to give the horse's back some added cushioning, even if only because the leather-lined saddle is colder to the horse's back when first put on and the numnah protects the leather from sweat and dirt.

A hunting breastplate is usually worn, but boots and bandages are omitted, for the same reason as in endurance riding, even though hunting also involves jumping.

Studs may be used when hunting, but the conventional way of shoeing hunters is with wedge and calkin hunter shoes on the hind feet. Hunter shoes — the familiar concave, fullered shoes — are the most commonly used shoes for riding horses for all purposes, but without wedges and calkins except when special shoes are required, as, for example, with driving horses. However, the importance of designing the shoes to suit the horse, taking account of his action and conformation, and to suit the purpose for which he is used, is being increasingly recognised. The use of wide-webbed shoes for endurance horses is a good example.

SHOWING

In showing classes your tack forms part of the overall impression which is being judged, and it is essential to have it correct for your class and of a style that will complement your horse and make him look his best. In ridden classes the basic tack is a double bridle and a show saddle. The bridle may vary according to your horse and your class; for example, a hunter or cob should have a workmanlike bridle, whilst a hack or riding horse can have a more showy bridle, with a coloured browband, stitched noseband and narrower leather. The heavier the horse, the thicker your bridle leather needs to be to make his head look in proportion. A pelham bit, with two reins, can be used as an alternative to a double bridle, especially if your horse has a small mouth.

Fig 94 Perfectly turned out for showing: Robert Oliver on the Champion hack, Rye Tangle.

Show saddles are made principally to show off the horse rather than for the comfort of the rider, being small, without too much stuffing and often with half panels rather than full panels. The seat is quite shallow and the idea is that the saddle should conform as closely to the horse's back as possible. However, remember that the judge has to ride your horse and he won't enjoy the experience if your saddle is uncomfortable. The flap should be fairly straight, but avoid saddles with flaps that are cut back or are so short that they interfere with the rider's boot.

The saddle should follow the same rules of fitting the horse as any other type of saddle. Your judge may be a tall man, so be sure to have leathers with enough room for adjustment and irons that are big enough. A hack or riding horse is best in a saddle with a straight flap, whilst a cob or hunter can have the flap slightly more forward cut. If you cannot afford a show saddle, an old-fashioned English hunting saddle is the next best thing. As the object of showing is to display the horse, numnahs should be avoided, and if you must use one, it should be kept as unobtrusive as possible. For working hunter classes, a straightforward general-purpose saddle may be used, and a snaffle bridle, with or without a running martingale, is permitted.

If you are showing in hand, an in-hand bridle looks smart (but is not essential if you are not planning to go to many shows). You can make one up using a leather headcollar with a browband added and a bit with leather buckle attachments, or you can simply use a snaffle bridle. For showing, brand new, light-coloured tack detracts from the horse's appearance, so try to use tack that is 'well run in'; if you have to use new tack, buy the darker-coloured leather and treat it several times with saddle soap and leather preservative before going into the ring.

There are many ways in which paying attention to detail can improve the appearance of your horse and maximise his chances in the ring; some of these will be considered in Chapter 12.

12 . Grooming, Presentation and Turn-out

Some owners spend more time grooming their horses than riding them; others just about spare the time to scrape off the worst of the mud with a dandy brush before riding.

Why do we groom horses?

1. To improve the horse's health and comfort: grooming removes dirt and waste products from the skin and coat, keeps it clean, and helps to stimulate better circulation, which discourages external parasites and helps prevent diseases of the skin.
2. To improve the horse's appearance by making him look clean and healthy.
3. To aid fitness, using strapping, banging and massage as a means of improving circulation of the blood and toning up muscles.
4. Grooming each day gives an ideal opportunity of checking the horse's general health and condition and spotting any minor injuries or abnormal aspects of his appearance which might otherwise have gone unnoticed.

The amount of grooming you should do depends greatly on how you keep your horse and the amount of work he is doing. A horse being rested at grass in the summer needs little or no grooming, apart from regular attention to his feet and perhaps something to help keep the flies away. In winter, a grass-kept horse who is not working should have the mud brushed out of his coat regularly and be closely watched for problems such as mud fever and rainscald. The stabled horse needs regular and thorough grooming, especially if he does not have the chance to go out to roll and shake loose hair and scurf from his coat.

A working horse at grass needs the natural grease in his coat to keep him warm, so should only have surface mud and dirt removed, whereas the stabled horse will be kept warm with rugs and blankets and can have his coat kept thoroughly clean, which makes for ease of management, especially if he is clipped. The most difficult situation to cope with is when you want to work your horse off grass, as many people do. In summer, when the horse has a short coat, the problem is not too difficult to deal with and the occasional bath on a warm day will not do the horse any harm, as long as you take care to see that he is thoroughly dried off afterwards; if necessary, rug him at night for a day or two until he gets the natural grease back into his coat. You might want to bath him, for example, if you are going to a show or competition.

In winter, you will have to accept the fact that grooming is harder work if you are working your horse off grass than if he is stabled. The most practical approach is to give the horse a trace clip, which will remove the thick hair from his chest and belly, where sweat and dirt otherwise accumulate, and will also prevent him sweating so much when he is working. Too much sweating leads to a loss of condition, and the horse may more easily catch a chill if he gets cold after exercise. A trace clip will help prevent this whilst leaving the horse a reasonable covering of hair to keep him warm. If you want to tone up his muscles and if he goes out rugged, a thorough wisping (*see* page 117) after exercise will help get rid of the sweat and improve his circulation.

GROOMING EQUIPMENT

Your grooming kit should contain the following essential items:

Dandy brush
Rubber curry comb
Body brush
Mane comb
Two sponges
Sweat scraper
Hoof pick
Hoof dressing and brush
Scissors, needles and thread or rubber bands

Additional useful items include:

Stable rubber or fabric grooming mitt
Water brush
Metal and plastic curry combs
Plaiting comb
Massage pad
Rubber grooming glove
Cactus cloth
Hoof pincers and buffer
Clippers and trimming clippers

Uses

The dandy brush is the basic item of equipment used for grooming grass-kept horses. It is a stiff brush which removes surface mud and dirt from the coat, without stripping the layer of protective

Fig 95 Grooming kit (left to right, back): water brush; fly repellent; shampoo; body brush; sponge; sweat scraper; kit box containing towel, hoof dressing and brush and grooming mit; plastic, metal and rubber curry combs. (Left to right, front): dandy brush; three types of hoof pick; plaiting comb; mane comb; scissors.

grease that builds up to help keep the horse warm and his skin dry. It should be used with short, brisk strokes. Being stiff and hard, however, it must be used with care on thin-skinned horses, some of whom will not tolerate the use of a dandy brush at all. Never use it on the head, nor on the mane and tail, as it will pull out the long hairs.

Dried mud can be more easily removed with a rubber curry comb, which does not seem to irritate thin-skinned horses as much as a dandy brush if gently used in a circular motion. A rubber curry comb is also extremely practical for removing loose hair, used in the same way, when the horse is slipping his coat. A rubber grooming mitt performs the same function.

Cactus cloth — a rough, open weave material — is good for removing sweat and stains.

The body brush performs the real business of cleaning the coat of the stabled horse, and it is worth buying the best you can find. It is a soft brush, with short, dense hairs, designed to penetrate to the skin and remove dust, grease and scurf, at the same time stimulating the sebaceous glands to produce oil and put a shine on the coat. To obtain the best results, the body brush should be used vigorously, with short strokes in the direction of the lie of the coat, and it should be cleaned every half-dozen strokes by scraping it against a curry comb. A rubber curry comb can double up for this purpose, or you can use a metal one, but the metal type should never be used on the horse. The curry comb can be knocked on the floor or wall to shake out the dirt.

The body brush is used on all horses to groom the head, mane and tail. Be very careful when grooming the head. Undo the headcollar and, provided your horse will stand quietly, rebuckle it around his neck while you groom his head. Brush his head in the direction of the hair growth, and be careful not to startle him when you raise the brush, nor to knock the bony areas with the hard back of the brush.

Brush out his mane and tail gently, separating out a few hairs at a time and being careful not to pull them out, especially from the tail. A mane comb is made of metal and has large, fairly wide teeth. It can be used gently to comb out a severely tangled mane — always start at the ends and work up to the roots, to avoid pulling out too much hair — but its primary use is when pulling your horse's mane (see page 117). A plastic curry comb is also useful for combing mud out of a tangled mane; again, don't pull out too many long hairs.

A plaiting comb has shorter, finer teeth than a mane comb and is used for separating the mane into sections for plaiting.

A water brush has longish, soft hairs and is used for damping the mane and tail to make them lie flat, or before plaiting.

Your two sponges should be kept separately, one for cleaning your horse's eyes, mouth and nose, the other for the area under the dock. Dampen the sponge, then wipe the eyes first, followed by the muzzle and nostrils; similarly, dampen the second sponge to clean the dock. A sponge is also useful for removing grass or dung stains on a light-coloured horse.

A sweat scraper is a curved metal or plastic blade, usually with a rubber insert, used like a squeegee for removing excess water from the coat after bathing or washing down.

One of the most important items in your grooming kit is the hoof pick, used for cleaning out your horse's feet each morning and again after exercise. It is particularly important to pick out the stabled horse's feet every day, as they become packed with dung and soiled bedding, which quickly softens the sole and frog and leaves the way open to the unpleasant fungal infection known as thrush.

Pick up the feet as described in Chapter 8 and use the point of the hoof pick to clean out mud, stones or soiled bedding that may have accumulated. Work from the heel of the foot towards the toe, to avoid digging the hoof pick into the leathery, V-shaped pad known as the frog. Run the hoof pick along the clefts of the frog to make sure all the debris is removed. Some hoof picks have a small, stiff brush incorporated, which is useful for making sure that nothing has been missed. As you pick out the foot, examine it carefully for any signs of damage to the frog or sole. The surfaces of both frog and sole grow with the foot and flake away, so a frog that has a flaky

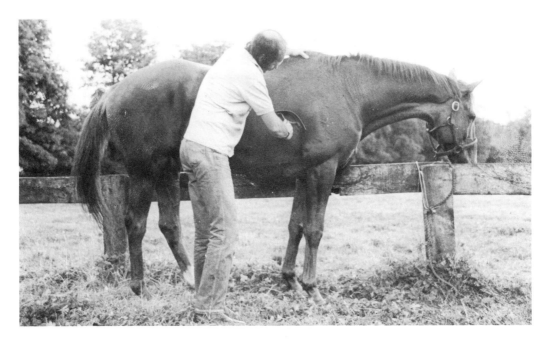

Fig 96 A wash down after work, using the sweat scraper to remove excess water.

Fig 97 Picking out feet, into a skip.

Fig 98 Picking out the foot, using the hoof pick in the direction of the toe.

appearance is quite normal. Deep cuts, or penetration into the sole that sometimes occurs from sharp stones, may need treatment and if they are dealt with quickly, the risk of infection will be minimised.

To stay healthy, the horse's foot needs to retain the correct moisture level. If the horse is kept in conditions that are too wet, the horn becomes soft and crumbly, if too dry it becomes brittle. Hoof dressings can be used to provide a waterproof barrier to prevent the passage of moisture in either direction: to help guard against softening of the horn and cracked heels if the horse is out in winter and, conversely, to prevent the stabled horse's feet from drying out. If a horse is permanently kept in, it may help to wash the feet, to replace lost moisture, before applying the hoof dressing.

Whether or not hoof dressings have any other useful effect is debatable. The best kind are those with a base of natural animal oils, lanolin, for example, which may help the horn to retain its suppleness and discourage cracking. Hoof dressings do not promote growth, nor make the horn stronger. The proprietary dressing Cornucrescine is often used to encourage growth in damaged feet and it does this by acting as a mild blister.

DAILY GROOMING ROUTINE

In principle, your horse should be groomed twice a day, before and after exercise. The first grooming is simply to tidy him up, remove mud and dust from his coat, sponge his eyes, muzzle and dock (although this is often omitted), pick out his feet and check him over before you ride him. This grooming is known as 'quartering', as it involves going over each quarter of the horse in turn. If a horse is stabled, it should be done each morning when his rugs are removed, to make him comfortable before replacing the rugs.

The second grooming, known as 'strapping' is done after exercise when the horse is warm, the pores are open, and scurf and dirt can more easily be removed from the skin. Strapping is the thorough grooming given to working horses who are kept stabled for a good proportion of the time.

As has already been mentioned, grass-kept horses should not be strapped.

Tie up the horse fairly short and begin grooming as usual with the dandy brush to remove mud and sweat, then use the body brush to remove dust, scurf and grease, cleaning it on your curry comb as you go. The mane and tail can also be brushed out with the body brush — its softer hairs will separate the strands without pulling out the long hairs.

Next, you will need a massage pad or a 'wisp', made by twisting hay into a rope and plaiting it to form a small, hard pad, which is dampened and used to massage the horse. The massage pad or wisp is used on the large muscle areas of the body only, that is, the triangle of the neck in front of the withers and towards the poll, the shoulder muscles and those of the hind quarters. The method is to bring the pad down on the muscle area with a firm 'bang', (hence it is known as 'banging), and to massage in the direction of the hair growth. Never bang the loins, which are sensitive, nor the bony areas of the body. The purpose of banging is to stimulate the circulation, aid correct muscle development and put a shine on the coat. It is a traditional method, widely used by producers of show and competition horses, and it takes considerable energy on the part of the groom. The number of 'bangs' applied to each area can gradually be built up from about 20 to 100 or more.

Finish your strapping by sponging the eyes, muzzle and dock (in geldings, the sheath may also need sponging out with water occasionally), picking out the feet, and applying a hoof dressing, if used, to the sole, frog, bulbs of the heel and the hoof wall. As a final touch, you can lay the mane with a water brush and go over the coat with your stable rubber (a linen cloth like a tea towel) to remove any last traces of dust.

PRESENTATION

Pulling

There are various ways of improving your horse's appearance for showing, competition, or simply to make him look smart. Conventionally, some horses, such as Arabs and native ponies, are left with their manes and tails free and full-flowing (Arab horses can have an Arab plait for competition work, to keep the mane neatly out of the way). Other horses have their manes pulled for neatness and to make plaiting easier, and their tails either pulled or plaited. A pulled tail cannot be plaited as the hair is too short, so you must decide which is most suitable in your case. If your horse is living out it is better to leave his tail unpulled, as it gives protection from the weather.

Most horses become quite easily accustomed to having their manes and tails pulled, but proceed with caution when you do this job for the first time − if the horse becomes upset it will be difficult to overcome his dislike of the procedure. The most important thing is not to pull too many hairs at once. Begin at the poll; you may need a stool or bale to stand on if your horse is tall. Comb the mane free of tangles, then pull a few hairs at a time, either with your thumb and index finger, or by wrapping them around a comb. Always pull the longest hairs first and always pull from underneath the mane. Never pull any short hairs that may rise from the crest on top of the mane as you will end up with a short, bristly regrowth that is impossible to control. If there are short hairs at the crest, either lay them with a damp brush or train them to lie flat by plaiting.

When pulling, work down towards the withers, keeping the mane an even length as you thin and shorten it. Pulling might sound like hard work and uncomfortable for the horse, but if you pull the mane after exercise, when the pores are open, the hair will come away fairly easily. Never cut the mane with scissors or clippers as it will not lie flat and you will be left with a ragged, unnatural looking finish. You can pull your horse's mane to whatever length you wish, but for plaiting, about four inches (ten centimetres) long is considered convenient.

The tail is pulled in similar fashion. Stand to one side and pull the hair on the opposite side to minimise any risk of being kicked. If you think your horse is likely to kick, get someone to hold him so that you can reach his tail over the stable

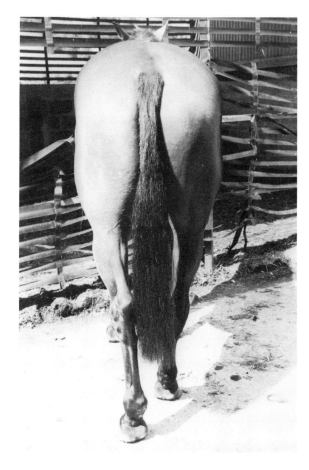

Fig 99   A neatly pulled tail.

door. Again, always pull from underneath, down the sides of the dock, and never pull more than a few hairs at a time. The tail should be pulled to about two-thirds of the way down the dock. If you are starting with a completely unpulled tail, it is advisable to pull it in two or three sessions, rather than try to do the whole job in one go, to prevent the horse becoming irritable and restless.

Trimming

Except with Arabs and native ponies, most horses have their tails trimmed straight across, or 'banged' at the bottom. Raise the tail, with your arm under the dock, to its naturally carried position, then trim straight across with sharp scissors at the level of the chestnuts, just below the hocks. This may be easier with someone to raise the tail for you if your horse is tall. Alternatively, but less commonly, the tail can be left switched, that is, pulled to a natural point.

Ears can be trimmed, if desired, by holding the edges closed then trimming neatly from point to base. Never remove the hair from inside the ears as it protects them from dirt and flies. Heels should be trimmed with a comb and scissors, taking care to do the job neatly and leaving enough hair to give some protection. Rain water runs down the long hair at the back of the legs and drains off, thus protecting the skin, so grass-kept horses should not be trimmed.

Plaiting

Plaiting is done to improve the horse's appearance for shows and competitions and needs practice to achieve a neat result. Traditionally, seven plaits was the correct number for a mane, but this is now more flexible and the basic rule is that you should have an odd number of plaits to achieve a balanced appearance. The greater the number of plaits, the longer the neck will appear.

Comb out the mane and divide it into an odd number of equal sections, securing each with a rubber band. Begin at the poll, by dividing the first section into three and plaiting from the roots as tightly as possible. There are several ways of finishing a plait. One method is to incorporate a length of thread into the plait, then loop it around the end of the plait and pull it tight, before doubling the plait under and sewing firmly into place. Finally, the thread should be knotted to secure the plait and the ends snipped off with scissors. As an alternative to sewing, rubber bands can be used to secure your plaits, although they do not stay in place as well as sewn plaits. The plait should be doubled under twice to give a neat appearance.

Plaiting the tail also takes practice and is difficult unless the dock hairs are fairly long. To begin, either take a strand from the centre of the dock and plait into it from the sides, or take two smaller strands from the sides and secure them together with a rubber band, to form the first

Fig 100   Plaiting the mane: (a) divide the hair into equal bunches;

(b) braid the bunches, starting at the poll;

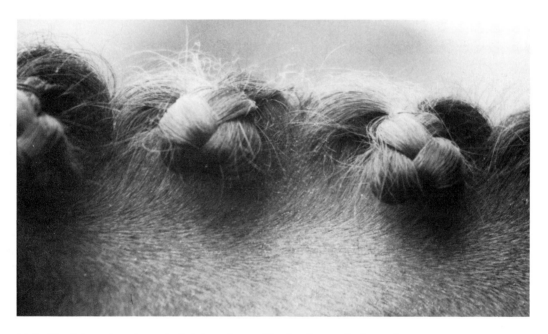

(c) double plaits under twice and stitch into place; rubber bands may also be used.

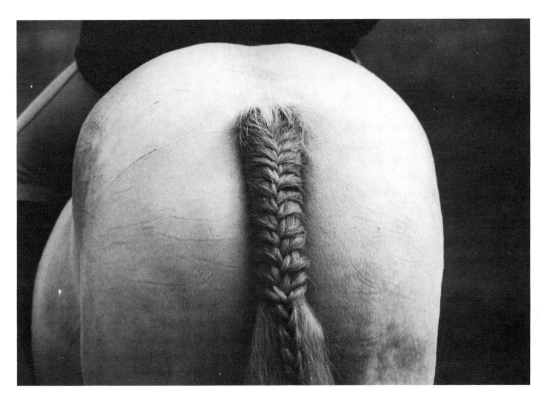

Fig 101   Plaiting the tail takes practice.

centre piece, again plaiting in from the sides. Take up hair in small sections from the sides and centre of the dock to plait in as you work down, so as to achieve a tight plait down the centre. From two-thirds of the way down the dock, plait the longer hair into a pigtail, which can then be turned under and sewn into a loop.

BATHING AND WASHING DOWN

The only real need to bath your horse arises if you want him to be particularly clean and shining for the show ring. The most important consideration is to see that he does not catch a chill, so make sure he is thoroughly dried off afterwards and avoid bathing him on a cold or windy day, if possible.

Always use a recommended animal shampoo for bathing, as it is specially formulated to avoid any harmful effects to the horse's skin and coat. Use tepid water, not hot water which would open the pores and may allow dirt to penetrate the skin. Always be sure to rinse off shampoo thoroughly.

Using a soft brush or sponge, work the shampoo into the coat (follow the manufacturer's instructions regarding dilution of the shampoo), starting at the poll, including the mane and working back towards the quarters. When shampooing the head, be careful not to get shampoo into the horse's eyes, nor water into his ears. Work down the foreleg, under the body and down the hind leg. Repeat the procedure on the other side. Shampoo the tail − immersing it in the bucket is the easiest way − and rub the hair between your hands to lather out the dirt.

Using a sweat scraper, remove the lather and dirt from the coat − the metal or plastic side is used on the body and the rubber side on the bony areas. Draw the sweat scraper along in the

121

direction of the hair. Thoroughly rinse off the remainder of the shampoo, then use the sweat scraper again to remove the excess water from the coat. Dry the horse's ears, legs and heels with a towel. Drying his ears will help keep him warm and drying his legs and heels will prevent the chance of chapping.

On a warm, sunny day, the horse can be walked dry. On colder days he should be lunged until dry, or thatched with straw. If your horse is dirty and sweaty after exercise and you wish to sponge him off, avoid the large muscle areas, as cold water on these areas can lead to muscle cramps. Sweat can be sponged from the saddle and girth areas, using as little water as possible, but it is preferable to brush off mud and sweat when the horse is dry.

CLIPPING

Many owners clip their own horses and once you have learned the technique it is not too difficult a task, the main requirement is patience, as it does take a little time to achieve a good result. If you have never clipped before, get an experienced person to show you how it is done; in any event, the job really requires an assistant to help with the awkward bits, such as between the front legs.

The horse in winter grows a thick coat, which is an inconvenience if he is expected to work hard. It causes him to sweat excessively, which leads to loss of condition and possible chills, if he gets cold whilst wet and sweaty. Sweat and mud also cling to the long hair, making it more time-consuming to groom the horse and keep him clean. The horse is therefore clipped. He will build up an extra layer of fat to help compensate for the loss of his coat, but he should also be kept rugged for warmth.

The trace clip is useful for horses kept at grass with a New Zealand rug. The racehorse clip is an alternative, preferred by some owners, which also leaves a considerable amount of the coat on the body, and with this clip the head may be clipped out or left unclipped, as desired. The blanket clip is the next stage up, leaving a blanket shaped covering over the body, plus the legs unclipped. The hunter clip is a complete clip with the exception of the legs, head and saddle patch, whilst in a full clip, the coat is completely removed. In most clips, the legs are left untouched to afford more protection against knocks, thorns, and other hazards, whilst leaving the saddle patch on in the hunter clip helps guard against a sore back.

Method

Various types of clippers are available, the most convenient and practical being the portable electric type. Clippers require careful maintenance to function correctly, so follow the instructions and keep them oiled and clean, with the blades sharp and at the correct tension. Also follow the safety precautions − connect the clippers to a safe power point and never use the clippers on a wet horse or in wet conditions.

Most horses can be clipped without too much trouble, but if you are not sure how your horse will react, be careful not to upset him. Prepare to clip in a clear area, with room to move around, and do not let the electric lead drag on the ground. Have an assistant to hold the horse and provide a hay-net to distract him. When you know he does not object, he can be tied up to be clipped. The horse must be clean to be clipped, as if he is dirty, the blades will quickly become blunted and the job will be more difficult. Mark out the clip on the horse with chalk, making sure it is even on both sides. Switch on the clippers and lay your other hand on the horse's shoulder, so that he can feel the vibrations of the machine. When he has accepted that, begin clipping at a flat area, such as the shoulder.

Clip against the lie of the hair, moving the clippers steadily in long strokes without pushing, but keeping them flat against the coat. Clip the body first, then the legs, and lastly the head. To clip behind the elbow, and inside the opposite leg, have an assistant raise the foreleg. It is also a good idea to have a foreleg lifted whilst you are clipping inside the hind legs, to minimise the chance of kicking.

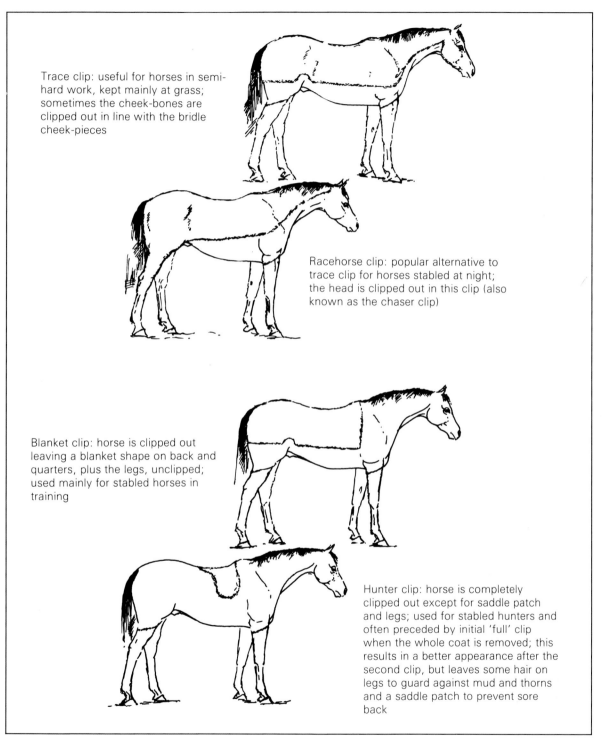

Trace clip: useful for horses in semi-hard work, kept mainly at grass; sometimes the cheek-bones are clipped out in line with the bridle cheek-pieces

Racehorse clip: popular alternative to trace clip for horses stabled at night; the head is clipped out in this clip (also known as the chaser clip)

Blanket clip: horse is clipped out leaving a blanket shape on back and quarters, plus the legs, unclipped; used mainly for stabled horses in training

Hunter clip: horse is completely clipped out except for saddle patch and legs; used for stabled hunters and often preceded by initial 'full' clip when the whole coat is removed; this results in a better appearance after the second clip, but leaves some hair on legs to guard against mud and thorns and a saddle patch to prevent sore back

Fig 102 Types of clip.

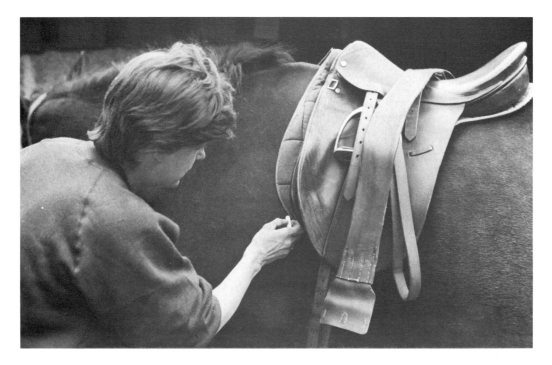

(a)

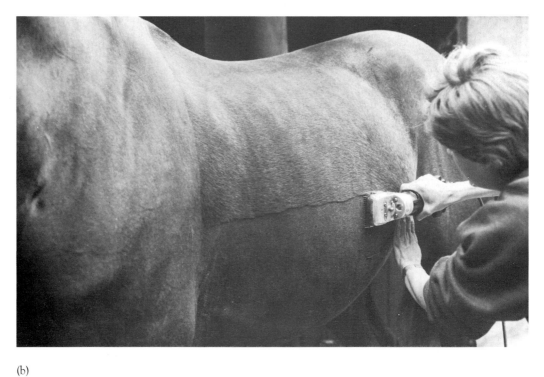

(b)

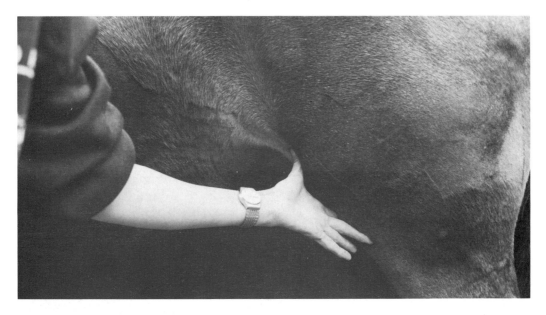

(c)

(d)

Fig 103 Clipping: (a) marking out the saddle area with chalk; (b) clip against the lie of the hair; (c) and (d) measuring the line of the clip at the top of the leg.

If the horse becomes restless and difficult, it is better to restrain him with a twitch than to become involved in a battle.

After clipping, groom the horse with a body brush to restore the oil to his coat and rug him to keep him warm.

125

13 . Fitness Training for Competition

Before you embark on any programme destined to get your horse fit, ask yourself the question 'What is the purpose of getting him fit?' The answer will have a considerable bearing on your choice of the right training programme and how you put it into practice. The level of fitness necessary, and the way the muscles are developed and used, varies according to the horse's competitive activities — for example, a show jumper needs a different type of training and level of fitness from a point-to-pointer.

The second thing to remember is that a horse's fitness does not depend only upon doing a certain amount of work each day, but upon all aspects of how he is managed and spends his time. It is therefore a prime concern of the stable manager.

If a horse is fed and exercised at the minimum level to keep him healthy, this represents management at a 'maintenance' level. If, however, you wish him to achieve a higher standard of athletic performance, such as in competition, you have to increase his capacity for energy production and utilisation. This is achieved by giving him more energy-producing food and increasing his work-load, so that a degree of stress is introduced.

Stress is necessary in order to achieve an improvement in performance, but if too much stress is applied, the result is distress. Distress may be evident in many ways: the horse may take an unacceptably long period to recover from his work, with an elevated pulse and, possibly, respiration rate; he may become exhausted and dehydrated, with the added complication of colic; or he might experience muscle cramps or tying up. Alternatively, he might simply damage himself through the effort of forcing tired muscles to go on working.

BODY SYSTEMS

To understand how to care for a horse during training, it is necessary to appreciate how his body systems work and what can be done to achieve the maximum improvement whilst avoiding the dangers.

All the body systems have a part to play in this process. The digestive organs — mouth, throat, gullet, stomach, small and large intestines — make up the alimentary canal which runs the length of the body and through which food is processed. Digestion of the different foodstuffs takes place at various stages along the way, much of it in the intestines, and is a continuous process in keeping with the horse's nature as a grazing herbivore. This should always be remembered when working out a feeding schedule, particularly with regard to competition horses, whose intake of the bulk food that keeps the digestion working may be limited. The job of the digestive system is to convert what the horse eats into a form in which the body can store it, either fatty acids or glycogen, until it is needed to produce energy.

Oxygen is also needed for energy production and is provided through the respiratory system. The cardio-vascular system carries the oxygen and food nutrients in the blood to the muscles, where energy is produced. The muscles use the energy they generate to expand and contract, thus mechanically moving the joints by way of the tendons and other connective tissues. Messages from the brain, communicating through the central nervous system, control and monitor the whole process.

All the body systems must function efficiently for fitness training to be successful and it follows

126

Fig 104   Different types and levels of fitness for different purposes:
(a) showjumping – strength and suppleness; (b) dressage – suppleness and the
health and sparkle that make 'presence'; (c) eventing – speed and stamina;
(d) endurance riding – sustained performance, strength and stamina.

that anyone concerned with fitness training should consider the condition of the whole horse and tailor the training programme accordingly. It is also essential to maintain a flexible approach and adapt the programme if necessary. For example, if the horse has an illness or is injured, there will be a set-back in training and work must be built up again gradually, once the horse is fit to resume his training. Perhaps your training programme does not progress as expected − the horse might not achieve the level anticipated in a given period of time, or he might progress faster. Beware of the latter, especially with a keen, forward-going horse, as there will be a temptation to do too much too soon.

ENERGY PRODUCTION

The aim of training is to increase the horse's ability to produce energy efficiently. Energy can be produced aerobically (using oxygen), or anaerobically (without oxygen). In any work both methods are used: the aerobic method mainly when work is slow and prolonged; the anaerobic method when fast bursts of energy are required.

Horses have two main types of muscle fibres, known as slow twitch and fast twitch. Fast twitch fibres are subdivided into FTa and FTb types. Slow twitch and FTa fibres can utilise oxygen efficiently, whilst FTb fibres are better able to produce energy anaerobically. Studies in exercise physiology have shown that the number of each type of fibres found in individual horses is probably a genetically determined factor and therefore some individuals are hereditarily more likely to do well in sports which require short, sharp bursts of energy, such as sprinting, whilst others will do better in sports which require stamina and endurance.

The anaerobic method of energy production uses glycogen as fuel and produces lactate as a side effect. When the glycogen stores run low and the lactate build-up is excessive, fatigue results. The situation can be delayed as training increases the tolerance of hard-working muscle fibres to higher levels of lactic acid.

Aerobic energy production depends upon the body's ability to utilise oxygen and this has been shown to be improved by increasing the amount of exercise given to the horse in terms of frequency of work periods, duration of each work period and the intensity of the activity in each work period. Increasing the work-load in this way can also be described as the application of increasing amounts of stress.

Obviously, the horse must not be over-stressed. The build-up of work must therefore be gradual and co-ordinated with the increase in energy-producing food (concentrates) and the horse's general health and condition.

TRAINING PROGRAMME

Preparation

A horse needs a basic level of fitness at which he can be ridden safely and in a balanced manner, in order to begin further training for any specialised sphere of equestrianism. The training programme to achieve this basic level is similar for all horses, subject to age, starting condition and previous level of fitness. A young horse whose muscles have never been hardened off must be taken considerably more slowly than an older horse who has previously been fit and is being brought back into work after a rest.

Before beginning any training programme, attend to your horse's routine health matters, making sure he is in the best condition to start work. A horse who is in poor condition and 'ribby' should be given a chance to build up his bodyweight before being asked to work at all.

Teeth should be checked, routine vaccinations attended to, feet trimmed and shod and the horse wormed. It is best to arrange any vaccinations during a rest period, as the horse should not be worked for a week after an influenza vaccination. Any changes in management should be introduced gradually. If the horse has not been used to hard feed, start with very small amounts and watch his condition carefully. If he is stabled, it is best to give him hay ad lib during early training, as he will have been accustomed to grazing freely in his field, and the hay-net will keep him occupied and help prevent boredom.

Bring the horse in for part of the day – either day or night according to the time of year – to begin with. (If you are training for spring events, he will probably have been in during the night in winter in any case.) Even if you plan to keep him permanently stabled during his training, do turn him out for at least a couple of hours a day, to allow him to relax. Some time to himself in as natural an environment as possible is very important to the horse's mental state and can make a considerable difference to his attitude to his work.

Early Stages

Your early training programme will begin with walking, to get the horse's muscles used to work and to harden off his legs. As with the human athlete, slack, inelastic muscles and soft tendons

and ligaments are more prone to injury.

The period of walking will be determined by the individual horse's starting condition. Traditionally, young horses were driven in long reins as part of their early training. This was an invaluable method of hardening them off without the encumbrance of a rider, as well as introducing them to new objects and experiences, but the practice seems to have been largely discontinued, probably because of the increase of fast traffic on the roads. The average riding horse will require about two weeks of walking, before progressing to slow trot work.

In the early stages of training, the horse is more likely to injure himself through clumsiness, or from 'spooking', than he is later on, as well as being in soft condition. It is therefore advisable always to use some form of leg protection, either bandages or brushing boots and, if much roadwork is done, knee boots are a good idea.

After the first two weeks, lungeing can be introduced, as an excellent means of suppling the

Fig 105   Rest and relaxation are also important.

Fig 106 Lungeing, a useful exercise in early fitness training or when the horse cannot be ridden.

muscles. This should be limited to ten minutes a day at first, increasing to no more than half an hour for a fit horse. Always lunge equally on both reins, to avoid an uneven build-up of muscle. Lungeing puts considerable stress on the joints and it is essential to have a level area with an even surface on which to work. Lungeing is also a useful way of exercising a horse who needs to work but cannot be ridden for some reason, for example, a sore back.

After two more weeks of walking and steady trotting — trot uphill only, as trotting downhill puts extra strain on the tendons and joints — slow canter work can be introduced. Short, sharp canters are not what is required at this stage, although hacking country often offers opportunities for this. Try to find a stretch of up to a mile, preferably level or slightly uphill, and teach the horse to canter steadily and rhythmically, without racing. Half a mile is enough to begin with, and the distance can

gradually be built up in conjunction with the horse's schooling. Cantering will both raise the heartbeat and increase the flow of air into the lungs, helping to improve the functioning of both the cardio-vascular and respiratory systems. However, at this early stage, cantering twice a week is quite sufficient.

Around the fourth week of basic training, mounted schooling can also be introduced, concentrating on exercises to stretch the horse's muscles and make him more supple. Work at the walk on a fairly long rein, with plenty of turns, plus steady trot work on large circles, with frequent changes of rein, is enough to begin with. Concentrate on having the horse relaxed, rhythmic and balanced, with good impulsion, using his back and quarters to push the power through from behind. Do not worry about collection at this stage, but allow the horse to work in a reasonably long, low outline.

After six weeks of work the horse should be

130

Fig 107   The stud horse also needs to be kept fit. Irish Draught Silver Jasper is
regularly ridden and hunted.

approaching a basic level of fitness. Throughout training, never underestimate the value of steady walking, especially up and down hills. It is the exercise least likely to cause damage and at the same time produces an increasing degree of underlying fitness and strength. In earlier times some of the fittest horses were the travelling stallions who were walked from district to district to visit mares. Equally fit were the men who walked with them, and if you want to improve your own fitness for riding, you could do worse than dismount occasionally, give your horse's back a rest and run alongside.

Interval Training

Interval training is much advocated and does seem to produce good results. The basic principle of interval training is to apply a specific amount of stress for a given time, for example, canter for three minutes, allow the horse almost to recover, then repeat the exercise several times. Trainers develop their own favoured routines for interval training, usually a combination of cantering and trotting, or cantering and walking, the aim being gradually to increase the amount of exercise, or stress, in comparison with the time taken for the horse to recover.

The effect on the horse can be assessed by observation, or more accurately measured using an electronic heart monitor — a device which displays the horse's heart rate whilst he is in action. Another method of assessing improvement in performance is to take the horse's pulse rate on finishing exercise, and noting the time it takes to return to normal. Obviously, as the horse becomes fitter, this time should be reduced.

Warming Up and Down

Whenever you exercise your horse, remember the importance of warming up and warming down. Cold, stiff muscles are as likely to sustain injury as slack, unfit muscles, so always spend a few minutes walking, then doing rising trot on a free rein, to loosen the horse up and get him warm. At the end of exercise, he needs to cool off gradually to prevent stiffening up and the risk of muscle cramps and chills. Always walk the horse gently after fast work or strenuous exercise, until he is cool and relaxed. Don't let him get cold − rug him if necessary − and on cold days use an exercise sheet on a clipped horse doing slow work.

FEED

The way you feed your horse during training makes a considerable difference to his performance. The basic rules of feeding remain the same, and as your horse becomes fitter, you will increase the amount of concentrates in his diet. Exactly what you feed, and when, will be something you will work out from experience, based on what seems to suit your particular horse best.

However, the first golden rule is to increase the amount of exercise in advance of the increase in feed, and if the horse has to stop work, or has his work-load reduced, his hard feed must also be reduced immediately, to avoid the risk of azoturia when he is brought back into work (*see* Chapter 15). The reason why azoturia is more likely to occur in these circumstances is uncertain at present, but it does appear to be linked to diet and exercise. (For a sample work and feed programme for a 15.2 hh. horse in basic training, *see* Appendix II.)

The question of how much bulk to feed is a difficult one, as the horse in his natural, healthy state consumes more bulk than a horse doing fast or strenuous work can be allowed. The only course is to monitor it according to the horse's work-load and condition. Developing an eye that recognises the horse's continually changing condition is an essential part of fitness management.

As with the human athlete, training will be geared to achieving peak performance on a specific day, with a gradual build-up of work before a competition, followed by a winding down period and a rest, to rebuild and restore the body's reserves before the next build-up.

14 . Travelling

Once you have a horse, sooner or later you will want to take him somewhere in a horse-box or trailer. This is a procedure that can be fraught with difficulty unless the horse is properly trained and the exercise approached in a methodical and safe way.

Whether you are travelling with a motorised horse-box, or a towing vehicle and trailer, make sure that the vehicles are in good order and that proper maintenance has been carried out. Check tool kits, jacks and spare tyres, and if you are using a trailer, check that the floor is sound. Also make sure that your vehicles conform to any transport or highway regulations.

CLOTHING AND PROTECTION

Your horse needs clothing for travelling, to protect him from injury, to keep him warm on cold days, or to keep him clean on the way to shows on warm days. For warmth, a day rug over an anti-sweat rug is usually sufficient. On hot summer days, the day rug can be replaced with a summer sheet, or a cooler can be used instead, to avoid marks from an anti-sweat rug being left on the coat. Whilst travelling, rugs should be fastened with a roller to prevent them slipping off. On warmer days the day rug can be quartered back, keeping the back, loins and quarters covered, but leaving the chest and shoulders free.

Leg protection can be either boots or bandages. Boots are more convenient to use, especially those that incorporate hock and knee protection as an all-in-one boot. However, carefully applied bandages probably give more support to a young horse, or to a horse on a particularly long journey who will have to stand for several hours, barely moving. Hock and knee boots complete the leg protection if the all-in-one type are not used.

When you consider how much time and energy it takes to prepare your horse for an event, and the potential for injury inherent in loading, travelling and unloading, it is not worth the risk of travelling without suitable leg protection. Some owners take the added precaution of putting on overreach boots to protect the heels of the front feet if bandages are worn, whereas many leg pads and proprietary travelling boots also cover this area.

The tail also needs protection, from rubbing against the trailer ramp, or side of the horse-box in transit, especially if your horse is inclined to lean back for support. A tail guard over the tail bandage will give extra protection. Many owners do not bother with a poll guard, but if you have a young or excitable horse, or one who is inclined to throw his head in the air it is a good idea to protect his poll.

LOADING

If you buy a well-schooled riding horse, it is to be hoped that he will also load easily and will not present you with any travelling problems. However, even with a horse who loads easily and calmly, it is important to follow the correct procedure, as the most equable horse can easily be put off loading and travelling.

Be sure that everything is ready in advance, and your car or horse-box packed and ready to leave. Have your travelling vehicle parked on level ground, or better still, facing downhill, so that the slope of the ramp is as shallow as possible. The floor of the vehicle should be suitably covered with straw or shavings, for the comfort of the horse and, if it makes loading easier, the partition in a trailer can be moved across until the horse is loaded. The breast bar should be in position and a loop of twine fixed to the tie ring, ready to tie up the horse.

Fig 108   The trailer is backed up to the barn and the gate forms a barrier to prevent escape on that side.

Fig 109   The lunge line can help a handler load a reluctant horse without assistance. Here the lunge line has slipped down a little too far — ideally it should be kept higher, around the horse's quarters.

Fig 110   Once the horse is loaded, the breeching strap is fastened to prevent him backing out.

Fig 111   Unloading at the rear of the trailer – be sure to keep the horse straight.

Fig 112   With a front-unload trailer the horse can walk out forwards – again be sure to keep him straight and do not let him rush out too fast, or he might be in danger of injuring himself.

If you are travelling only one horse in a two-horse trailer, load the horse on the side nearest the centre of the road: in Great Britain on the right, in the United States, on the left. The weight of the horse helps counteract the effect of centrifugal force in conjunction with the camber of the roadway and gives greater towing stability. It is also better to travel with the partition in place so that the horse is confined to one side of the trailer; otherwise, in moving about in the trailer, he might cause swaying and instability.

When all is ready, lead the horse straight towards the ramp and up into the trailer. A trained and obedient horse should have no hesitation in loading. It is advisable to have an assistant who can fix the partition, put the breeching strap across and raise the ramp as soon as the horse is inside. Otherwise, you will have to tie the horse up first, then quickly go round and get the ramp up. With a well-behaved horse this should be no problem, but many horses are quite

capable of running backwards out of a trailer if they feel so inclined.

Tie up the horse short enough for safety, but long enough for him to be able to keep his head and neck straight. Provide a hay-net to keep him occupied during the journey.

Before setting off, make sure that the trailer, if you are using one, is properly attached to the towing vehicle, and that all doors are fastened and all equipment securely fixed. Also check that all your lights and indicators are working correctly.

If you are embarking on a long journey, see that your horse has water available until the last moment before loading. Always give a horse a chance to digest his food before starting a journey – feed him earlier than usual if necessary.

Loading Problems

A young horse who has never been loaded, or an older one who has developed a dislike of the procedure, needs careful handling, the former to ensure that he is not given cause for fear, and the latter to overcome his resistance.

The rules are:

1. Stay calm.
2. Be fully prepared in advance.
3. Don't be in a hurry – the job might take all day.
4. Practise loading the horse before it becomes necessary to take him on an actual journey.
5. Organise the session so that you have two assistants to help you.
6. Be positive and don't give up until you have achieved your goal.
7. Make your preparations thoroughly, so that everything is ready before you take the horse out of the stable.

First, park your vehicle so that the access into it is as easy as possible, on level ground or facing downhill with the ramp lowered uphill. The ramp must be firmly down on the ground, so that it provides a solid footing when the horse steps on to it. Weight it down or pack underneath it, if necessary. Also park so that the possibilities for escape around the sides are minimised, for example, in a lane entrance, or alongside a wall.

See that the breast bar is in place (in the case of a trailer), move the partition over to make the opening wider and more inviting and, if there is a front ramp, lower it to allow in more daylight. Some horses will load more readily if they can see right through a trailer. With a trailer which will unload at the front by removing the breast bar, it is possible to walk a horse right through and out

Fig 113 Loading for the first time. The lorry has been backed into a lane entrance and the ramp liberally spread with straw.

again, then take him to the back and reload. Doing this several times might help to give him confidence in the whole procedure. Spread some straw or shavings down the ramp to make it look more familiar to him.

Dress the horse for travelling – injuries can happen just as easily whilst practising loading as on a journey. To give yourself more control, put his bridle on over the headcollar. Have ready a bucket with some feed, probably nuts which you can easily offer from your hand, and a lunge line.

Lead the horse straight towards the back of the ramp and speak to him encouragingly as you go. Behave confidently and firmly as though you expect him to walk in. He may do so. However, if he has never been loaded, or has learned to object, he will probably hesitate when he reaches the ramp. In this case, don't rush him. Let him sniff at the ramp, then quietly encourage him forward again and offer him the bucket of food. Give him a mouthful from your hand and keep encouraging him forward. At this point, if he refuses to step on to the ramp, one of your assistants can carefully lift his front feet, one at a time, until they are on the ramp. If the ramp is solid, this is often enough and the horse will go the rest of the way, although it may take several minutes more.

If he backs off, or refuses to go forward, repeat the procedure until the front feet are again on the ramp. Stay very calm. Ask your assistants to stand one each side of the horse and link hands behind his quarters. Each time the horse relaxes, the assistants should push him forward, whilst you encourage him at the front. Most horses do not kick, but your assistants should be ready to move out of the way quickly if the horse does kick out. This method is usually effective, but it is most important to stay calm and avoid upsetting the horse.

If only one assistant is available, or if the horse is inclined to kick, a lunge line can be used, attached to one side of the trailer and looped around the horse's quarters. The assistant takes up the strain on the lunge line each time the leader urges the horse forwards; this also discourages the horse from moving backwards off

the ramp. If necessary, one person can load a horse alone using this method, although help is advisable if you are loading a difficult or untrained horse.

Some people achieve good results by giving a horse a tap with a lunge whip, or even a yard broom, as he hesitates before entering the box. This can work well with horses that are simply stubborn, but should not be tried with nervous horses, who may very well kick out against the whip and fight any attempt to drive them into a box. There are also special gadgets devised as assortments of ropes and pulleys, which can be used on reluctant loaders, although these should not be necessary if the correct procedure is followed calmly and firmly.

Failing other methods, if you have a safe enclosed yard where you can leave your horse-box with the ramp down, the horse can be kept without food for a period, then left in the yard with his feed inside the box (be sure that trailers are stabilised so they will not tilt forwards or backwards when the horse steps on to the ramp). Sooner or later, the food will tempt him in. Whatever method you choose, patience is the key.

THE JOURNEY

How good a journey the horse has will depend greatly upon the skill of the driver. Towing takes practice, and if you are new to travelling horses in this way, it is a good idea to take an empty trailer to a safe place and practise before setting out on a real journey with a live load. Remember that if you are towing, acceleration will be slower than usual, whilst braking distances will be longer. Good anticipation is vital. Always keep a safe distance from the vehicle in front of you and pull away and stop as smoothly as possible. Be aware of the length of your vehicle and allow enough room to turn; also be aware of the height of the vehicle and allow for overhanging trees, pulling out to avoid them if necessary. Keep to the speed limit and change down gears to go downhill, in the same way as you would to go up. A trailer is more stable when it is actually being pulled along by the towing vehicle, rather than cruising along freely behind.

Anticipation, allowing yourself plenty of time to deal with hazards, is the key to successful towing. In this way, you will not only give your horse a more comfortable ride − braking smoothly, keeping going slowly where possible and avoiding sudden stops and starts − but you will also save wear and tear on your vehicle and trailer.

On a really long journey, stop periodically to give the horse a rest, water and feed. If possible, take him out to stretch his legs for a few minutes before going on to your destination, but be sure it is safe to do so, and don't unload if reloading is likely to be a problem. Don't travel for more than about four hours without offering the horse a drink.

ARRIVAL

On arrival at your destination, unload the horse using the loading procedure in reverse. Give him a chance to look at his new surroundings, then take him to his new stable, if appropriate. At a show or event it is easiest to leave the horse in the trailer or horse-box until he is needed to warm up for his class. Afterwards he can be tied up outside the box, but do not leave him tied up unattended.

Remove his travelling clothes and check him over for injuries. After a long journey, your horse will appreciate a drink, a hay-net and being left alone to rest.

15 . Common Ailments

What happens if your horse becomes sick or injured? This is often the cause of the leisure horse owner's greatest worry, yet most problems can be satisfactorily treated, with the minimum loss of use, provided prompt and appropriate action is taken. The first rule when you notice something wrong is not to panic. Assess the situation calmly and, if you have any doubt about the nature or severity of the problem, call your veterinary surgeon.

Some problems, such as severe injuries or symptoms of acute pain, obviously need fast expert attention; others are less easy to define and it is sometimes tempting to delay calling in professional help. This can be a false economy, as well as being unfair to the horse, as early attention will frequently prevent the development of a much more serious condition. The second rule, therefore, for dealing with illness or injury, is to treat the problem as quickly as possible. It is not really difficult to decide when it is necessary to call the vet; if your horse is unwell or injured and you do not know *exactly* what should be done, you should seek qualified assistance.

The third rule is to follow your vet's advice and treatment instructions fully and precisely. You might be tempted to discontinue treatment if you think the horse is better, but if your vet has ordered a specific course of drugs or other

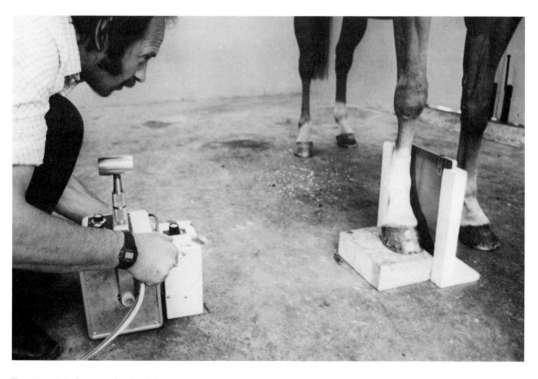

Fig 114   Modern methods of diagnosis, such as X-rays, mean that most problems can be quickly identified and the appropriate treatment recommended.

treatment for a specific period, that is what should be given. In any event, you will still have to pay the bill.

Don't be put off asking questions if you don't understand what is wrong, or why your vet has prescribed or carried out a particular form of treatment. You are entitled to know, and most vets will willingly explain what is happening to an interested client. Similarly, if you are unsure how to give any prescribed treatment, ask the vet to show you what to do. For example, you may have to give a series of daily injections, or change wound dressings. It is not unknown for owners to fail to carry out treatment because they cannot cope with what is required, but are afraid to ask for help.

WOUNDS

Minor wounds are the most frequently occurring injuries with which the horse owner is likely to be faced. They fall into four categories: contused wounds, or bruises; puncture wounds; lacerated wounds, where the tissues are torn; and incised wounds, made by a sharp cut, such as from glass.

Most bruises heal quickly and the process is aided by the application of cold to the bruised area. This can be by means of cold hosing (lower leg bruising is often helped by standing the horse in running water, such as a nearby stream), or the application of ice packs. If ice packs are used, the bruised area should be bandaged first, then the ice pack applied and held in place with a further bandage.

Puncture wounds occur more frequently than might be expected, especially in the feet, when infection is also almost certain to follow. Puncture wounds are characterised by deep penetration, but a small surface area, and the most important thing to remember is that they must be kept open and left to heal from the inside outwards, to allow for drainage. Initially, poultices should be applied for two or three days, to draw out any dirt. Traditionally poultices were made from bran, but the most effective now are the proprietary dressings, such as Animalintex.

With lacerated and incised wounds, the procedure is to stop the bleeding, clean the wound and apply a suitable dressing. Most small wounds can be adequately treated without veterinary assistance. Bleeding usually stops fairly quickly and the wound can be gently washed with a mild antiseptic solution. Keep everything, including your own hands, as clean as possible and use surgical cotton wool to bathe the wound. If dirt is lodged in the wound, remove as much as possible without probing. Finally, dress the wound with an antibiotic spray.

More serious wounds may need stitching and where there is a risk of infection a course of antibiotics may be recommended. Wounds involving joints, which can lead to serious complications with possible permanent damage, deep wounds, or those where foreign objects, such as wood or glass splinters, have become embedded, should always have expert attention. If you do treat a wound yourself, keep a close watch for any signs of infection or break-down in the healing process and call your vet at the first sign of trouble.

TETANUS

Whenever a wound occurs, however small and insignificant it might seem, check that your horse's anti-tetanus vaccinations are up to date and call the vet immediately if they are not. Tetanus is an extremely distressing disease. Some cases do recover, if caught early enough, but they are few and the disease is still quite common. It is caused by bacteria, which live in the soil as spores and which find their way into the horse, either through a wound, or, it is thought, through the digestive system. Deep puncture wounds, which may be tiny on the skin surface, are especially dangerous, as the bacteria thrive in an anaerobic environment, that is, when there is no oxygen present. They produce a toxin which affects the nervous system, reaching the spinal cord and the brain. The result is paralysis, slow at first, then more rapid, until the respiratory system is affected and death follows.

Fig 115   A serious wound that required skilled attention. The horse made a complete recovery.

The soil in many areas is heavily contaminated with tetanus. There is absolutely no reason why you should risk your horse catching the disease, as it is easily preventable by vaccination.

LEG INJURIES

The strength of a horse's legs and feet is vital to his performance as a working animal. In competition, the horse's tendons − the ropes of tissue which join muscle to bone − are put under considerable strain. When the tendons are unable to cope with the level of strain exerted, a rupture results. Similar injuries can be caused by a blow to the back of the leg as, for example, when a horse moving at speed strikes into himself. Tendon injuries take a considerable time to heal and complete strength may never be

regained. Treatment consists of anti-inflammatory drugs combined with continued cold applications, and, when the injury is no longer painful, by a long period of controlled, graduated exercise.

Problems can occur in the bones of the leg as well as in the tendons. One of the most common bone disorders, occurring in young horses up to seven years old, is the formation of splints. These become evident as swellings along the side of the cannon bone where it is joined by the splint bone. The swellings are soft at first, then become bony. The horse may be lame whilst the splint is forming, but unless the splint interferes with the horse's action (for example, if the growth is high under the knee), the lameness usually disappears.

Bone spavins, ringbone and sesamoiditis are other common conditions affecting the bones of the legs. They are all caused by strain and their

141

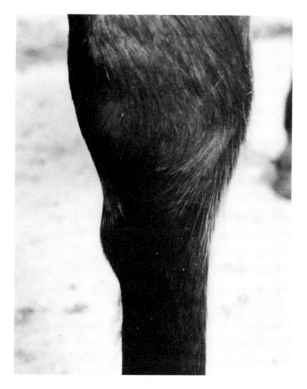

Fig 116 A splint. This one is high up and could possibly affect the action of the knee.

Fig 117 A curb.

seriousness depends upon the extent of the injury and, in the case of ringbone, whether the pastern and pedal bone joints are affected.

A curb is a swelling of the ligament at the back of the hock, due to strain. It is frequently found in young horses and will cause lameness in the early stage, which will usually disappear, although the swelling will remain. Bog spavin, thoroughpin and capped hocks are all conditions involving swelling of various parts of the hock, but which do not usually cause lameness. Wind-galls are small, soft swellings around the fetlock joint, often found in fit horses, and which usually disappear when the horse is exercised. They are technically a blemish, but not otherwise troublesome.

A fit, stabled horse may well suffer from 'filled legs' following a night's rest. The condition results from an accumulation of fluid in the lower limb, which disperses when the horse is exercised. Lymphangitis is a more serious condition involving painful swelling caused by infection of the lymphatic system, accompanied by a high temperature. Veterinary treatment is essential.

FOOT INJURIES

The greatest number of lamenesses arise from trouble in the feet, and the most serious common ailment affecting the feet is laminitis. This is usually found in fat ponies kept on lush pasture, but may also result from trauma to the feet, or retention of afterbirth in mares after foaling. There are now thought to be several contributory causes, including excessive carbohydrate intake, and various forms of infection, which lead to the onset of laminitis.

The condition itself involves damage to the

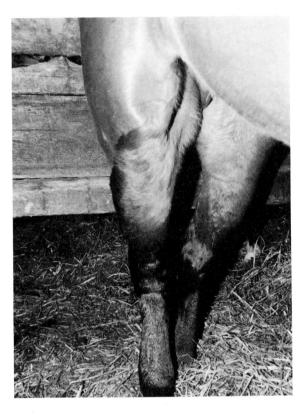

Fig 118 Lymphangitis.

laminae of the hoof, that is, the tissue which joins the hoof wall to the pedal bone. It is a painful disease and the horse will stand with his front feet pushed out in front of him (the condition usually affects both forefeet). Frequently, laminitis is not treated quickly enough — the long-term effects begin within a few hours of the onset of the disease, and drastic treatment, involving special shoeing and stripping away the hoof wall from the affected area, to allow new horn to grow down, is then required if there is to be any chance of a cure. Laminitis is always likely to recur, so careful management is needed to see that the horse is kept on a suitable diet.

Navicular disease is a degeneration of the small navicular bone towards the back of the foot. It is difficult to diagnose accurately and used to be considered incurable. However, recent advances in treatment and understanding of the condition

have had considerable success in controlling it and research indicates that prevention depends upon good foot care and maintaining a good hoof/pastern axis.

Sand cracks, or grass cracks, are splits in the hoof wall resulting from inadequate foot care and trimming of the hoof. Usually, if the crack does not extend up the full height of the hoof wall, burning across the top with a hot iron and trimming back the hoof at the base of the crack, coupled with regular trimming, will resolve the problem. With more serious cracks, the two sides can be laced and glued together and left to grow out. Providing the coronary band is not affected there is a good chance of recovery, but it will take at least six months for the new hoof to grow down.

DIGESTIVE PROBLEMS

Colic is the term used to describe the symptoms of abdominal pain, which may be due to a number of causes. A major cause is the blocking of an artery by worm larvae, with damage to a section of the gut and resultant acute, spasmodic pain. Other causes may include eating unsuitable food, changes in diet, bolting food, too much cold water immediately after exercise, a build-up of sand taken in by the horse when drinking from a stream, or exhaustion and dehydration. Cases of mild impaction (common in the United States, where grazing is often on sandy soils) can usually be cleared up by giving a purgative, but when a more severe obstruction occurs in the small intestine there is a danger of a twist and total blockage occurring. In this case surgery is essential, but the situation is still often fatal.

Fortunately most colics are spotted and treated quickly, with successful results. The symptoms are patchy sweating, pawing the ground, looking round and attempting to bite or kick the flanks, rolling, restlessness and shivering. The horse may lie flat out and his pulse and respiration will be increased. Some attacks are mild and pass off quickly, but in this situation it is best not to take chances and to call the vet immediately.

143

RESPIRATORY PROBLEMS

Dust

The importance of a dust-free environment to prevent the coughing and loss of performance associated with chronic obstructive pulmonary disease (COPD) or small airway disease (SAD), as it is now known, has been dealt with in Chapters 6 and 7. It has been established that the creation of a dust-free environment will overcome the problem, even in badly affected horses, but it should be stressed that the environment must be completely free of dust. Haylage must be fed instead of hay, and dust-free bedding, such as shredded paper, must be used. The horse must also be stabled away from other horses not kept under a dust-free regime, and from hay and straw stores. Turning the horse out as much as possible will also help. Thoroughly soaking hay reduces the airborne spread of spores and reduces the risk of SAD in less sensitised horses, but the spores are still present and soaked hay will not solve the problem for severely affected horses.

Viral Infections

The 'virus' is the nightmare of all commercial equestrian establishments and is the term commonly used to describe the group of infectious respiratory diseases, the most common of which is equine influenza. As has already been stressed, all horses should be vaccinated against influenza. It spreads very easily when infected horses are moved from one yard or area to another and the main symptoms are a high temperature, a nasal discharge and a cough. The condition can cause death in young horses, but the greatest danger is a secondary infection causing pneumonia. Complete rest is required and any horse found to be infected should immediately be isolated from others in the yard.

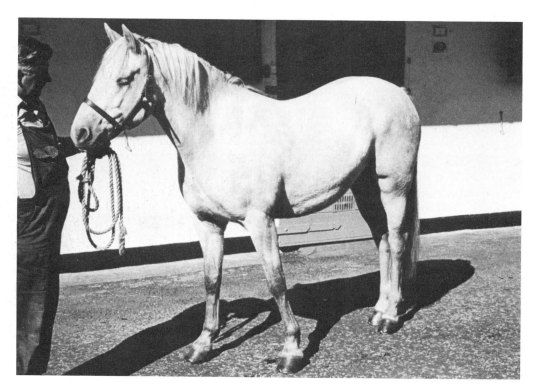

Fig 119 The 'heave' line along the horse's belly is a sure sign of SAD.

Strangles

Another common and extremely infectious disease affecting the respiratory system is strangles. It is caused by bacteria and is spread by contact with an infected horse, who may, in fact, show no signs of the disease himself. Symptoms are a sore throat and difficulty in swallowing, a high temperature and a thick nasal discharge, accompanied by the formation of an abscess on the glands between the jaws, which swells and eventually bursts. Once the abscess has burst, recovery begins and with good nursing the condition should clear up satisfactorily.

AZOTURIA

Azoturia is the most widely used name for the condition resulting from muscle damage, also known as Monday-morning disease, set fast, or tying up. The term 'equine rhabdomyolysis' is now commonly used in the veterinary profession to describe the condition. As already mentioned in Chapter 13, the precise causes of the condition are uncertain, except that they are linked to diet and exercise and how the two are combined. The symptoms are sweating, increased respiration and pain in the large muscles of the loins and hind quarters, which become hard and swollen, with the horse increasingly unable to move. The urine can become reddish or dark, containing myoglobin (the muscles' equivalent of haemoglobin), or even particles of muscle tissue. In severe cases these particles can clog the kidneys and cause renal failure – a condition with a high risk of death.

Fortunately, with prompt treatment and rest, most azoturia cases recover. If your horse develops azoturia, don't try to move him, but rug his loins and quarters to keep the muscles warm until the vet arrives. There is a tendency for the condition to recur, so always pay strict attention to diet and keep exercise ahead of food.

SKIN PROBLEMS

Skin problems may be due to infections, parasites, allergies or tumours. One of the most common infections, especially where horses are kept in old buildings which may also have been used by cattle, is ringworm. This can also affect humans, so it is important to wear protective clothing and thoroughly disinfect anything that comes into contact with the horse. The infection is spread by contact and is caused by fungi, which produce spores, which in turn spread and develop into the easily recognised groups of round scabs. Treatments by means of various antibiotics are successful and the important thing is to prevent the spread of the fungus.

Rainscald and mud fever are winter plagues caused by bacteria which thrive in wet, muddy conditions. They are prevented by good management, but if your horse does suffer from either condition, the remedy is to keep him dry, remove the scabs by gentle grooming (the hair

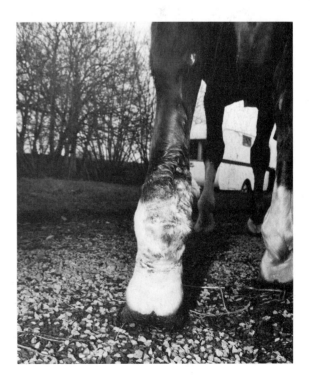

Fig 120   Mud fever.

will come away too) and treat the area with a mild antiseptic. For severe cases, your vet may prescribe a course of antibiotics.

Horses may occasionally be troubled by infestations of lice, which can be dealt with by dusting with proprietary louse powder. Other skin parasites include mange mites, which can affect horses with heavy feather; harvest mites which attack the pasterns of thin-skinned horses in late summer; and warbles, which are now fortunately rare in Britain, thanks to the government's campaign to get rid of the warble fly in cattle. Where warbles do occur in horses, they cause a large lump, usually in the saddle area, which may burst, like an abscess, but may need surgical removal.

For many years the cause of that annoying condition, sweet itch, was unknown, but now it is thought to be an allergic reaction to the bite of a particular species of midge. Sweet itch causes the horse intense irritation, hence the rubbing of the mane and tail until the hair is lost and the skin affected. As the midges are unlikely to stop biting, treatment to prevent and control the condition must be continued throughout the danger period, that is, the summer. Ideally, the horse will be brought in during the early morning and late afternoon, when the midges are at their most active. Various chemical lotions and washes are used, both to discourage the midges from biting and reduce inflammation and the extent of the damage to the skin. Insecticides are also used to kill the midges. These are sprayed over the horse and must be a type safe for horses recommended by your vet.

Urticaria is the name for sudden, extensive weal-like swellings which may appear all over the horse's body. It is related to sudden changes in the diet, or an allergy to some other substance which has been introduced into the horse's system. It

Fig 121   Sweet itch.

can be treated effectively with antihistamines, but it is important to identify the source of the trouble to prevent further outbreaks and more serious consequences.

Skin tumours of various types are quite common in horses and vary from fairly insignificant warts, which often disappear of their own accord, particularly in young horses, to the malignant melanomas found only in grey horses, which are ultimately fatal. Some tumours can be removed by surgery, but have a tendency to recur, so treatment is not always successful.

16 . Therapy and Folklore

In the final analysis, the purpose of stable management is to produce a healthy, fit and happy horse. With this purpose in mind, the owner's whole approach should be a positive one, with the aim of achieving recognisable results and preventing potential problems, rather than waiting for things to go wrong before taking necessary action.

THE HEALTHY HORSE

The healthy horse is a creature of habit – if he deviates from his normal behaviour, suspect that something is wrong. For example, if he does not look over the stable door and greet you as usual in the morning, but stands looking miserable in a corner, or if he spends far more time than usual lying down, or suddenly begins to drink much more or much less, he is probably unwell. A churned up bed, listlessness, loss of appetite and a dull or staring coat are all signs of trouble and the caring owner will sense immediately that all is not well, even before he has time to assess the situation in detail.

A healthy horse is an attractive picture, with bright eyes and an alert expression. His coat will be flat and shining, the skin underneath loose and elastic. His ribs will be well covered and his muscles, if he has been well schooled and got fit, hard and well developed. His legs will be clean (that is, free from any lumps or bumps), his tendons hard and cold, and his action free with a swinging stride and a spring in his step. The mucous membranes lining his eyes, nostrils and mouth will be pink and moist, his droppings will be smooth, moist and firm and his urine clear and pale in colour.

Temperature, Pulse and Respiration Rates

The vital signs of a healthy horse include his normal temperature, pulse rate and respiration rate. Taking his temperature is one aid to diagnosing illness. The horse's normal temperature is 99.5 to 100.5 degrees Fahrenheit (37.5 to 38 degrees Celsius) and it can be checked with a veterinary thermometer. Make sure the reading is well below 100 degrees Fahrenheit (37.8 degrees Celsius), grease the thermometer with Vaseline and, standing to one side of the horse, insert it into the rectum, rotating it gently. Make sure it touches the wall of the rectum and hold it in place for one minute before reading.

The normal pulse rate is between 36 and 42 beats per minutes, and the pulse has a rhythmic, two part beat. The pulse rate rises dramatically with exercise to well over 100 beats per minute during fast work, but should fall to around 60 as soon as exercise stops, then quickly return to normal. The pulse can be taken with a stethoscope, just behind the elbow, or using the fingers to feel the pulse where an artery passes over a bone close to the surface of the body, such as under the jaw.

Respiration should be soundless – any noise in the breathing when the horse is at rest indicates a severe respiratory disorder – and the normal rate is between 12 and 20 complete breaths per minute, though some horses manage to breathe even more slowly. The respiration rate can be taken by watching the horse's flank and counting, each in and out being a complete breath. Noisy breathing when the horse is exercised, except those breaths emitted when the horse breathes out whilst cantering, are indicative of respiratory trouble, which may have various causes. The endoscope, a modern instrument which enables the vet to see into the

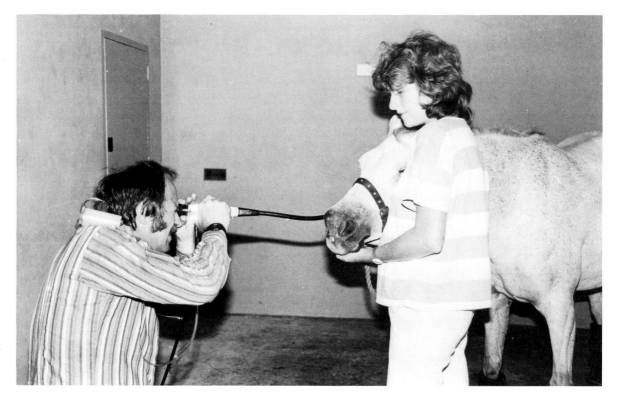

Fig 122   Examining the horse's respiratory system using an endoscope.

horse's respiratory system, has proved a major advance in diagnosing the source of respiratory disorders. 'High blowing', a snorting sound often made by Thoroughbred horses whilst cantering or galloping, has no adverse effect on performance.

NURSING

If your horse falls sick, or is injured and off work, nursing him back to health is basically a matter of common sense. Put him in the largest stable available, with a good thick bed right up to the door to prevent draughts. Keep the horse warm and dry. Unless otherwise directed, see that he has a good supply of clean water and a hay-net within reach. Any hard food should be drastically reduced, or omitted altogether, in line with the restriction on the amount of exercise the horse is permitted. If in doubt, ask your vet about diet and follow any recommendations he may make. If the

horse has to be kept stabled for a long period, offer fresh green food, such as lucerne or fresh cut grass (remove any uneaten grass before it wilts); succulents, such as sliced carrots and apples, can be useful in tempting a sick horse to eat.

Hygiene is important, especially if the horse is suffering from an infectious disease. Any utensils, clothing and other equipment used for the sick horse should be kept separate from that used for other horses, and washed or disinfected after use as appropriate. Keep feeding bowls and buckets clean. The same applies to grooming kit, although the sick horse is better left unbothered by too much grooming. Light grooming or gentle massage will help the circulation and the feet should be picked out daily. Bedding removed from the box of a horse with an infectious or contagious disease should be burnt.

When your horse has recovered enough to start work again, the process should begin very slowly. Illness will have a debilitating effect and the horse will need extra time to recover his normal strength and fitness before progressing further. Start with gentle walking, for not too long a period at first, and gradually increase the time to an hour a day. Turn the horse out if possible, so that he can relax, stretch his legs and get his body systems working efficiently at his own pace. When he has been back in work for a short time, the horse will tell you by his attitude when he is ready to work harder.

THERAPIES

Physiotherapy

Various forms of physiotherapy, many of them borrowed from human medicine, have been developed to aid the process of a return to full fitness.

Swimming has long been recognised as beneficial, as it allows the muscles, heart and lungs to work without putting any strain on the legs, whilst the water supports the bodyweight of the horse. There are many purpose-built equine swimming pools, but those lucky enough to live near the sea have an additional benefit, as apart from actually swimming, walking your horse through the waves at the shoreline will have a cooling and strengthening effect on his legs. In any case, taking your horse to the beach is a pleasure that need not be restricted to times when therapy is needed.

Chiropractic and Osteopathy

The services of equine chiropractors and osteopaths are widely available and are much vaunted by those who have found their treatment to have successful results. However, veterinary research indicates that the success of any such treatment is likely to depend upon its effect on soft tissues -- muscles and ligaments — and not on the bones themselves. It has been proved that horses do not displace vertebrae, nor do 'slipped discs' occur, and it is impossible to manipulate the bones in the horse's back.

Ultrasound and Faradism

Ultrasound is a technique which involves the use of very high-frequency sound waves to speed up the healing of damaged soft tissues, especially in tendons and ligaments. The sound waves penetrate the tissues and help reduce swelling and inflammation, break down adhesions and remove waste products. Ultrasound is also a valuable diagnostic tool. Used for this purpose, ultrasound equipment can display a 'sound wave picture' of the area of tissue concerned on a screen, enabling the veterinary surgeon to pin-point problems.

Faradism is another modern technique, used on muscles, both to diagnose problems and to aid a return to normal muscle function. It is based on stimulation by means of electrical impulses which cause the muscle to contract and relax rhythmically. Circulation to the area is improved, fluid is dispersed and adhesions between muscle fibres, resulting from previous injuries, are broken down.

Magnetic Therapy

Whilst ultrasound and faradism are proven beneficial techniques, magnetic therapy is a more recently introduced method of treatment, the efficacy and value of which needs further verification. It is based on the theory that the effect of the magnetic field is to realign damaged tissue into its normal healthy pattern and so promote faster and stronger healing than occurs when the tissues — for example, tendon or muscle fibres — are left in the tangled state resulting from injury. It is fairly widely used in commercial establishments and has been generally found to be of more use in helping with muscle injuries than tendon problems.

Massage

Massage is known to have a beneficial effect both in healing and developing muscles, by getting rid of tension and helping the horse to relax. There is much that the owner can do himself —

149

strapping is a form of massage, and massage using the fingertips can be as helpful to the horse as to the human. However, if your horse has been injured, or his performance is lacking and you think physiotherapy might help, seek your veterinary surgeon's advice in accurately diagnosing the problem. If your vet does not carry out the actual treatment himself, be sure to consult only a trained physiotherapist, whose knowledge is backed up by a thorough understanding of the horse.

Acupuncture

It has become fashionable recently, to indulge in the use of so-called 'alternative' medicine. Somewhere between this and conventional practice lies the art of acupuncture. This ancient Chinese method of treating all kinds of ailments has now acquired considerable respect in the West as an efficacious branch of medicine. There are trained acupuncturists within the veterinary profession and the method is sometimes used on horses, although more research is needed to establish its value in specific terms for the treatment of different conditions.

Herbalism and Homeopathy

Herbalism and homeopathy are still regarded as fringe medicine. The former is simply the application of the therapeutic qualities of various plants in treating different ailments, in the same way as modern science applies the use of chemical drugs. It has a long history and its exponents stress that its advantage lies in the use of 'natural', as opposed to 'artificial', ingredients. Many herbal remedies and food supplements are freely available for purchase for equine use, from comfrey for healing, to garlic as a tonic for the blood and to discourage flies.

Homeopathy works on the principle of giving tiny doses of a substance that actually causes the major problem, in order to develop an immunity.

The difficulty with both herbalism and homeopathy is the lack of comprehensive, scientifically proven data to substantiate the claims made in their support. This does not mean that these methods of treatment do not work, but it is difficult for the lay person, that is, the horse owner, to be sure that his or her money is being well spent.

FOLKLORE

Certainly modern veterinary science ensures that working horses of all types are better cared for today than they have ever been, and the body of equine knowledge continues to expand at a surprising rate, in view of the fact that man and horse have been intimate companions since the dawn of history. The importance of the horse in the history and evolution of human society is emphasised by the extent of myth, legend and mystery surrounding him.

To be a horseman was to command respect and if many of the traditional horseman's methods and theories have been outdated, disproved or simply lost, there are many that are still in common use, repeated and passed on from generation to generation. Some will swear by certain methods whilst others scoff at them. Some remedies are obviously barbaric by modern standards, others operate merely on faith or superstition.

One common practice that has quite recently been virtually discontinued is that of firing damaged tendons. This procedure involves influcting numerous small burns with a hot iron, and used to be thought to strengthen the healing tissue. After firing, a long period of rest was needed. It is now generally accepted that the rest alone would effect the same improvement and all the firing achieved was to see that the long period of rest was enforced.

Blistering involves the use of caustic substances to produce an inflammation supposed to aid healing. Blisters may be very mild or extremely strong and were usually used to reduce swellings such as splints, spavins and capped hocks. Blistering is still quite common, although there is considerable pressure for it to be discontinued, especially where strong blisters are concerned.

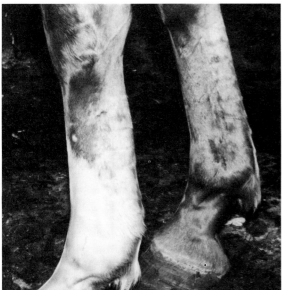

Fig 123   Fired tendons — the row of line scars is visible on each leg.

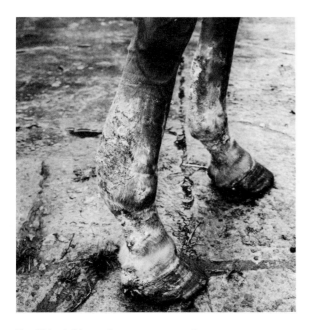

Fig 124   A blister that went wrong. A strong blistering agent was applied without the precaution of protecting the horse's pasterns and heels. Unsightly scarring is likely to be the result. Used here as an alternative to firing, the treatment was in any case unlikely to have any beneficial effect.

The use of goose grease as a blistering agent is unlikely to be found nowadays!

The tricks of the horse dealing trade, in days when a good pony could be bought for five pounds, were legion. Here are two which, it is to be hoped, no self-respecting dealer would use today, both told to my grandfather by a 'traveller'.

First, to deal with sweet itch, wait until the spring, when the mane and tail have grown and there is no sign of the problem. Then, ride your horse to a distant town, where he is not known, and sell him there. The drawback is that you will have to walk home, for if you buy another horse there, you might bring the same problem back with you!

The second trick relates to the horse with broken wind. It is to tie a camphor ball to the bit on the day before the sale, then, when the horse is sold, his problem will miraculously, if temporarily, have disappeared!

Along with the tricks, go the charms. Faith healing is by no means restricted to horses and there are those who believe in it and those who practise it still full of conviction today, although the number of those professing such gifts is rapidly dwindling. The charm may involve the repetition of some words or the laying on of hands. Usually the ailment is a growth of some kind that will not respond to other treatment, or an infectious disease such as ringworm. The power of faith is not something capable of scientific proof and horse owners must draw their own conclusions.

Certainly, when the horse was man's main source of power and transport, faith of another kind, coupled with superstition played a large part in horse lore. The power to control difficult horses was much respected and the methods of those who wielded such power were envied as closely guarded secrets. There were supposedly secret words, known only to the initiated, whilst other horsemen could control wild horses by talking to them with a special voice. Thus grew up the stories of the 'whisperers' and the 'horseman's word'.

Most curious of all was the special talisman

151

which identified the toadmen — a particular bone from the body of a natterjack toad or a frog. Kept about the person, it was supposed to give its owner power to handle any horse. An alternative use was to grind the bone up into powder and mix it with other substances to form an ointment which, applied to the horse, was said to give complete control over him. The most fascinating aspect of the whole process was the means by which such a bone was acquired. It was necessary to catch your frog or toad, hang it on a blackthorn bush to die and for the birds to strip its bones, then take the skeleton to a gently flowing stream and cast in the bones. One bone would float upstream against the current and this was the one you wanted. It was a forked bone, said to represent the shape of the frog of the horse's foot. Acquiring such a bone was not to be undertaken lightly as it was said to involve a pact with the devil, from whom, presumably, the desired power came. This was another practice, efficacious or not, that was handed down through the generations, and it is not beyond the bounds of possibility that in some rural corners of England, one or two toadmen exist today.

Finally, there is no doubt that the greatest friend of the horseman, traditional or modern, is known as 'Dr Green'. This book has consistently attempted to persuade you that your horse is healthiest and happiest when kept as close to his natural environment as possible; there is many a horse owner or vet who, shaking his head over a baffling problem, has decided to 'turn him out in the field and see what Dr Green will do'. Frequently, the improvement is suprising.

Perhaps that is a better reward for a good horsemaster than a row of silver cups: to take off the headcollar and watch your horse trot happily across the field on his own business; to lean on the gate and watch him prick up his ears and scan his surroundings, roll and shake the dust from his coat, wander in a leisurely fashion to see what may be on the far side of the hedge and finally settle down to the methodical grazing that indicates all is well.

Appendix I

ESSENTIAL VITAMINS AND MINERALS

Vitamins

	Sources	Uses
A	Good quality hay and grass	Needed for healthy bones, joints and mucous membranes and good eyesight
B Group		
Folic acid	Grass, silage and lucerne; a high cereal diet may be deficient in folic acid	Needed for healthy red blood cells; deficiency will cause anaemia
Biotin and methionate	Deficiencies may occur in a high cereal diet	Needed for development of healthy hooves and hair
Thiamine	An enzyme in bracken destroys thiamine	Needed for energy production; bracken 'poisoning' results in weakness, lack of co-ordination, prostration and coma
D	Production of vitamin D requires sunlight; adequate amounts found in well-made hay; also made in the body by the action of sunlight on the skin	Needed to regulate calcium and phosphorus absorption by the body
E	Found in high levels in cereals	Needed for healthy muscle development
K	Destroyed by an enzyme in clover	Needed for blood clotting, but overdose more common than deficiency; overdose causes kidney damage and failure

Note
Vitamins are required in only very small amounts and most vitamins are toxic if overfed.

Minerals

	Sources	Uses
Calcium	Found in grass, silage and good quality hay; cereals are deficient in calcium	Essential for healthy growth and development of strong bones
Phosphorus	High levels in cereals	Essential for healthy bone development
Magnesium	Adequate levels found in all foods	Needed for correct functioning of the nervous system

Note
In the high cereal diet of the stabled horse the correct calcium:phosphorus ratio of 1:1 to 2:1 is likely to be unbalanced, with the horse receiving insufficient calcium. Therefore a balanced supplement should be fed.

Trace Elements

	Sources	Uses
Copper Cobalt Selenium Zinc	Condition of soil determines amounts available in forage; deficiencies occur in some areas, but tiny amounts only are needed in the diet and trace elements are toxic if overfed	Selenium involved with Vitamin E in healthy muscle development; zinc may be needed for good hoof formation; cobalt and copper are essential for growth; copper and zinc interact resulting in copper deficiency where high levels of zinc are found

PROPERTIES AND USES OF FEEDSTUFFS

Bulk Food

Grass: forms main part of diet of horse living out and contains all essential nutrients in varying amounts, depending upon season.

Hay: main bulk food of stabled horses which provides fibre, plus other nutrients according to quality. Good quality hay is essential for horses. Poorly made hay may be dusty or mouldy, causing respiratory problems, or may be deficient in vitamins and generally of less nutritional value. Seed hay, cut from leys, also known as hard hay, has a higher protein content and is fed to working horses. Meadow hay, cut from permanent pasture, has a greater variety of grasses, is softer and generally of less nutritional value.

Ensiled hay or grass: made from hay or partially dried, cut grass, compressed and vacuum packed to retain maximum nutritional value. It is not dusty so is good for horses on a dust-free regime. It is also of higher food value than hay, so fewer concentrates may be fed.

Oat straw: good quality oat straw is palatable, provides fibre and is used in making chaff.

Chaff: A mixer for concentrate feed, to prevent the horse from eating too quickly. It is made of chopped hay, or equal parts chopped hay and oat straw.

Sugar beet pulp: available as shreds or nuts, which must be soaked for 24 hours in cold water (at least 12 hours if hot water is used), before feeding. If unsoaked sugar beet is eaten, it will swell in the gut, causing serious, possibly fatal digestive problems. Soaked sugar beet is a valuable bulk food, useful for putting on condition and as a mixer for cereals. Its high calcium level helps compensate for low calcium in cereals, especially oats.

Lucerne (alfalfa): high protein food which can be grown in small plots and cut fresh to give to stabled horses. Also used for high quality hay in the United States and for high protein ensiled hay.

Succulents: carrots, apples and other root crops, sliced lengthways, are a useful addition to the diet of stabled horses and as a means of tempting fussy feeders.

Bran: traditional mixer, now used less due to high phosphorus:calcium ratio and difficulty of obtaining good quality broad bran. Also used as a purgative in the form of bran mash.

Grass meal/nuts: useful for horses whose hay intake is restricted.

Concentrates

Oats: high protein cereal with easy digestibility, so a basic ingredient of equine concentrate diet. Low in calcium.

Barley: valuable cereal for putting on condition of show and performance horses. Less readily digested than oats so best fed cooked. Can be boiled at home or bought ready cooked as micronised barley.

Maize/corn: high carbohydrate food. Small amounts only should be fed. Useful for fussy feeders and horses who lose condition easily. Fed on cob, shelled or cooked and flaked.

Peas and beans: protein rich. Often used for

racehorses in hard training when quantity of food needs to be reduced without reducing energy value. Fed split or crushed.

Vegetable oil: fed to hard-working horses where stamina is needed, for example endurance horses. Provides high density energy and encourages fatty acid utilisation.

Linseed: raw linseed is poisonous to horses. It must be soaked for 24 hours, then boiled. When cool, jelly is mixed with feed. Protein rich and used mainly to improve coat on show horses.

Molasses: sweet derivative of sugar. Mix small quantity in warm water and pour over feed. Tempts fussy eaters or helps disguise medicine, etc.

Eggs: popular as a 'conditioner' for fit horses, before a competition. Must not be fed continuously as they contain a substance which destroys vitamins.

Milk: liquid, powder or pellet form. Used mainly for brood mares, youngstock and convalescent horses to build up condition.

Compound feeds: follow manufacturers' directions carefully. Do not mix with traditional feeds as this will unbalance the ration. May be in cube or coarse mix form. Provides balanced ration and is convenient to use.

Complete compound feeds: balanced ration including bulk. Difficulty is boredom for stabled horses, but useful for horses who cannot eat hay.

Appendix II

BASIC TRAINING

Below is a sample programme of work and feed for a 15.2hh. riding horse in basic training.

Week	Work	Feed
1	Begin walking half an hour building up to one hour roadwork by end of week	2lb (0.9kg) oats, 2lb (0.9kg) barley, 2lb (0.9kg) soaked sugar beet or chaff divided into two feeds; hay ad lib and turn out during day
2	Continue walking (roadwork) one hour a day, six days a week	Maintain feeding programme; increase hard feed if horse shows signs of losing condition
3	Introduce lungeing – 10 minutes only at beginning; continue walking one to one and a half hours a day, on and off roads, including short trots uphill	Increase hard feed to 4lb (1.8kg) oats, 2lb (0.9kg) barley, 2lb (0.9kg) sugar beet or chaff, divided into two; increase sugar beet if horse loses any condition
4	Continue on and off roadwork with walking and trotting; continue lungeing, building up to 20 minutes, i.e. 10 minutes each rein; total work-load one to one and a half hours a day, six days a week	Maintain feeding programme; include a broad spectrum supplement if desired
5	Commence mounted schooling, half an hour maximum at the start, continue fitness training, including slow uphill canters; total work-load as week 4	Increase hard feed: 6lb (2.7kg) oats, 2lb (0.9kg) barley, 2lb (0.9kg) sugar beet or chaff; if possible divide into three feeds, giving largest feed at night
6	Continue all training: e.g. day 1, roadwork; day 2, schooling; day 3, roadwork; day 4, cantering and off road work ; day 5, schooling; day 6, roadwork	Maintain feeding programme; horse should still be turned out each day and can live out or in, as preferred; grazing should be restricted if living out (keep horse off lush new grass)
7	Fast work and interval training can now be introduced, not more than twice a week; also gymnastic jumping, i.e. cavalletti and grid work; take care not to over-stress horse	Feed according to work-load and condition; if horse becomes too excitable, reduce oats; if lacking energy, increase oats; if overweight, reduce sugar beet and barley; if losing condition, increase sugar beet and barley
8	Progress into specialist training, but maintain flat work and fitness work-outs, also walking exercise	As fitness increases, hay/grass is traditionally reduced as hard feed is increased; however, horse must have enough bulk to keep digestion functioning well; a hay-net also helps prevent boredom when horse is stabled; hard feed should be increased to a level where horse maintains condition and performance without over-excitability or excessive weight gain; muscles should build up and size of gut will reduce as intake of bulk feed decreases

Useful Addresses

Arab Horse Society
Windsor House
Ramsbury
Marlborough
Wiltshire

Association of British Riding Schools
Old Brewery Yard
Penzance
Cornwall

British Driving Society
27 Dugard Place
Barford
Near Warwick
Warwickshire

British Horse Society
British Equestrian Centre
Stoneleigh
Kenilworth
Warwickshire

British Show Hack
Cob and Riding Horse Association
Rookwood
Packington Park
Meriden
Warwickshire

British Show Jumping Association
British Equestrian Centre
Stoneleigh
Kenilworth
Warwickshire

British Show Pony Society
124 Green End Road
Sawtry
Huntingdon
Cambridgeshire

Farriers' Registration Council
4 Royal College Street
London NW1 0TU

Hunter Improvement and National Light Horse
    Breeding Society
96 High Street
Edenbridge
Kent

National Foaling Bank
Meretown Stud
Newport
Shropshire

National Pony Society
Brook House
25 High Street
Alton
Hampshire

Royal College of Veterinary Surgeons
32 Belgrave Square
London SW1 8QP

Side Saddle Association
Highbury House
Welford
Northamptonshire

Society of Master Saddlers
Easdon
Lower Icknield Way
Chinnor
Oxfordshire

Weatherby and Son
42 Portman Square
London W1N 0EN

Further Reading

Black's Veterinary Dictionary, 15th edition (A. and C. Black Limited, 1985)

Haworth, J. *The Horsemasters* (Methuen London Limited, 1983)

Houghton Brown, J. and Powell-Smith, V. *Horse and Stable Management* (Granada Publishing, 1984)

Leighton Hardman, A.C. *The Amateur Horse Breeder* (Pelham, 1970)

Pavord, T. and Fisher, R. *The Equine Veterinary Manual* (The Crowood Press, 1987)

Rees, L. *The Horse's Mind* (Stanley Paul, 1984)

Rose, M. *The Horseman's Notebook* (Harrap Limited, 1977)

Rossdale, P. *Horse Breeding* (David & Charles, 1981)

Index